Out of INDIA

Contemporary Art of the South Asian Diaspora

December 8, 1997 – March 22, 1998

Essays by

Jane Farver, Curator

Radha Kumar

Queens Museum of Art
New York City

Out of India: Contemporary Art of the South Asian Diaspora
is sponsored by Bell Atlantic.

This exhibition and related educational programs are supported by public funds
from the Office of Queens Borough President Claire Shulman, the New York
State Council on the Arts, and the New York Council for the Humanities.
Additional funding has been provided by The New York Community Trust,
The British Council, and Anheuser-Busch Companies.

The Queens Museum of Art is housed in the New York City Building, which
is owned by the City of New York. With the assistance of Queens Borough
President Claire Shulman and the New York City Council, the Museum is
supported in part by public funds from the New York City Department of
Cultural Affairs. Additional funding is provided by the New York State
Legislature and the New York State Council on the Arts.

Queens Museum of Art
New York City Building
Flushing Meadows Corona Park
Queens, New York 11368-3398

Design: Linda Florio Design

Contents

Acknowledgments

My first encounter with India was as a child growing up on a farm in rural Virginia. My father's cousin had just returned from a Fulbright fellowship in India. Her recollection of people, sights, and sounds sparked in me an awareness of a world beyond the horizon of pastureland in the foothills of the Blue Ridge Mountains. Slide projections captured the brilliant hues of the marketplace, forming one of my earliest visual memories. India revealed to the nine-year-old in the 1960s the vista of another world, yet the array of works in the current exhibition *Out of India: Contemporary Art of the South Asian Diaspora* presents a far richer experience encompassing not only the Indian subcontinent but also many other lands and cultures.

The 27 artists represented in the exhibition and their families have lived in an amazing breadth of locales since the independence of India and the formation of Pakistan in 1947. Paralleling this diaspora in South Asia, the United Kingdom, Africa, the Caribbean, and North America have been rapid advances in telecommunications with both the corresponding ability to maintain contact with friends and loved ones left behind as well as shared access to global broadcasts of current events. The result is a wealth of perspectives and identities proffering insight into the complexities faced by global citizens worldwide.

Out of India exemplifies the goal of the Queens Museum of Art as it strives to present art of relevance to the people of New York City and, especially, the borough of Queens. In the metropolitan area are an estimated 350,000 persons who trace their heritage to the Indian subcontinent. Simultaneously, the 1990 U.S. Census characterizes Queens as the most ethnically diverse county in the country, and implicit in Museum exhibitions such as this one are the acknowledgment and encouragement of a multitude of perspectives and cultures making up our local community as well as our global society.

Bringing together works from several continents has entailed the generosity of numerous contributors and lenders. Major grants were received from the New York State Council on the Arts, a State agency, and the Office of Queens Borough President Claire Shulman. We also wish to thank corporate sponsor Bell Atlantic, and Alana Kennedy and Bill Martin whose assistance and understanding have been most appreciated.

Out of India is the largest exhibition to date of works by artists of the South Asian diaspora, and many individuals and organizations have contributed to this ambitious project. We are grateful for the counsel of knowledgeable advisors from the earliest planning stages which has assured an exhibition of commendable depth and scope: Ambassador Prakesh Shah and Mrs. Veenu Shah, Sigrid Burton, Daniel Dion of OBORO, Barbara Hunt, Geeta Kapur, Suzy Kerr, Peter Nagy, Director of Nature Morte New Delhi, David Chandler, Gilane Towadros, and Paola Barbarina of INIVA, Diana Nemiroff, Curator, National Gallery of Canada, the staff of *Panchayat*, Chandrakant Pancholi, and Mark Sealy of Autograph.

We extend our congratulations to the artists whose special insight is particularly meaningful in an era of vast migration and transience, as revealed by Radha Kumar in her personal account comprising the catalogue essay. The generosity of lenders and the coordination of overseas loans has truly made this project possible; our thanks are due to: Jacquelyn and Bruce Brown; Shireen Gandhy, Gallery Chemould; H.V. Goenka, RPG Enterprises Limited; Aliya Hasan; Joseph Havel; Chester and Davida Herwitz; Rakhi Sarkar, Centre of International Modern Art; and Nima Poovaya Smith, Cartwright Hall, Bradford. We are indebted to His Excellency Harsh K. Bhasin, Consul General of India in New York, and D.K. Paliwal, Consul of Education and Culture, for special assistance. The exhibition catalogue has been greatly augmented through the expertise of Linda Florio, designer, and Anne Schneider, editor.

I would like to take this opportunity to thank the Museum's Board of Trustees and President Constance B. Cooke who continually demonstrate enthusiastic support for exhibitions which embrace the diverse cultural heritages of Queens. Jane Farver, Director of Exhibitions at the Queens Museum of Art, must be credited for envisioning this first-of-its-kind project, and its realization reflects the professionalism of the staff of the curatorial department: Hitomi Iwasaki, Arnold Kanarvogel, Carol Potter, Bill Valerio, and interns Sachie Kimura and Tanya Rose. The preparation and presentation of every exhibition and related interpretive programming requires the professional skills and tireless commitment of our staff. We thank Assistant Director Marilyn Simon, Curator of Education Sharon Vatsky, Controller Mary Brown, Assistant Director for Corporate, Foundation, and Government Relations Kerry McCarthy, Public Information Officer Robert Mahoney, Facilities Manager Lou Acquavita, Manager of Museum Services/Chief of Security Tony Kemper, and members of the Museum's Business, Development, Education, Facilities, and Security Departments, as well as a corps of devoted volunteers.

Carma C. Fauntleroy
Executive Director
Queens Museum of Art

Home Base India?

by Radha Kumar

One of my favorite pieces of Indian English is related in a story my mother tells of two Tamils meeting at a concert of Carnatic music. In the interval, one turns to the other and asks, "Enjoying?" "Simply!" comes the ineffable answer, with a happy wag of the head.

My grandmother was always uncomfortable when my mother told the story. Why make fun of Tamils to the English? Her own grandmother had thrown away a dinner set after her husband brought an Englishman home to dine; the outcaste's touch polluted not only the dishes he touched but the dishes from which the family ate and the dishes in which the food was cooked. By the time my mother grew up, however, first in Lahore and then in Bombay, English had become her chief language, as it had for my father, sent off to boarding school at the age of seven. My parents met as undergraduates in England and married in Dehra Dun, a hill resort in north India; their circle was the cosmopolitan nationalists who were going to build independent India. While they were not in the first or even second generation of middle-class Indians educated in Britain, they were among a still relatively limited number. Perhaps what marked my parents' generation of "England-returned" from the earlier generations was how many more of them were nationalists.

Their marriage was unusual in more ways than one. My father came from the northern state of Uttar Pradesh, while my mother's family came from the southern states of Tamil Nadu and Karnataka. His family was richer than hers, but his caste was inferior to hers — she was a Brahmin and he a Vaishya. Their marriage caused consternation on both sides, but after a few years he became the favorite son-in-law of my Tamil relatives while she was esteemed as the educated daughter-in-law by my UP relatives. Nevertheless, they were different from most of the other couples in their families, and the third family they had, that of cosmopolitan friends, was not a sufficient cushion to the irritants each sometimes found in the other's cultural foibles. My father's UP laxity with friends and family exasperated my mother, while her sharp Tamil tongue riled my father.

As a child, my mongrel descent allowed me to seek refuge from one set of relatives in another, although the tolerance of my UP family was more attractive than the vigilance of my Tamil family. When both became simply too much family, I turned to my parents' anglicized New India — by now a Delhi circle of writers, bureaucrats, journalists, academics, and company executives — as a marker of my difference. But what seemed to many of my cousins an enviable choice of play left me with

uncertainty rather than an easy multiculturalism. From quite early on, I began to suspect that I suffered from ill-digested fragments of identity. This suspicion was strengthened when, at the age of fourteen, I went to England for a year. On my first day at the Cambridgeshire grammar school, a kind classmate, whose task it was to ease me into those unfamiliar environs, confided that until I had arrived, the "darkest" person she and the others had ever seen was an Israeli girl, the only other foreigner in the school. Home, I began to think, was not so much a point of departure as one of involuntary return.

The question faded when I returned to Delhi. Ill-digested as my identity might seem from time to time, the decades in which I grew up, the 1960s and early 1970s, were ones in which it was enough to be a Delhiite. To my friends and me that meant to speak in an argot in which "Don't be funny!" meant "Don't be stupid!"; to consider punning among the higher forms of wit; to walk in the Lodhi Gardens, a walled complex of weathered tombs on grassy knolls between tree-lined avenues; to buy used books at the Sunday pavement sales by the walls of the Red Fort; and to eat *parathas* (a kind of stuffed, fried wholemeal pita) in parathewali galli, an alley of the old city. Our first jolt came with Prime Minister Indira Gandhi's declaration of a State of Emergency in 1975, and the bulldozing of poor homes in the old city, but the shock ebbed fairly quickly when the Emergency was lifted in 1977. The big jolt came in 1984, after Mrs. Gandhi's assassination, when there was a pogrom against Sikhs across northern and parts of western India. Two of Mrs. Gandhi's Sikh bodyguards were accused of murdering her, in retribution for the army invasion of the Sikh holy shrine, the Golden Temple at Amritsar, during her regime.

The real figures of how many died in less than a week of mayhem will probably never be known. The official toll was roughly ten thousand dead in the country; just under two thousand died in Delhi. We who had gone into burning alleyways and run refugee and rehabilitation camps believed the figure to be much higher. And while there is limited equivalence between literal death and the death of a spirit, the sight of men on fire — with lit tires around their necks — shattered the Delhi which had allowed me to reconcile my north and my south, and my west. That sense of loss became the individual death of my innocence, though I shared it with thousands of Delhiites — the argot speakers and punsters — who had poured out of their homes to try and stop the riots, in an almost visceral assertion that this was our city, accreted through five different empires, a city that had resolved in the aftermath of a partition which had claimed countless victims, including Mahatma Gandhi, that never again would such terrible sights be seen in the Delhi streets.

In the immediate aftermath of the riots, Sadat Hasan Manto's *Toba Tek Singh* became the metaphor of communal loss to an entire generation that had grown up believing in the "never again" vow. Set in a lunatic asylum during partition's frenzy, the story uses a series of familiar inversions to point up the terrible wrenching displacements partition caused. In the asylum, as news spreads that the insane are to be divided, along with the sane, between India and Pakistan, the lunatics debate what these new places India and Pakistan can possibly be. Wild speculations abound, but the fact that these could be communally defined territories occurs to no one, and when the story's protagonist, Bishan Singh, asks where his village will be, in India or Pakistan, no one in the asylum can guess. Outside the asylum, when he lines up on the new border, many of the officials know but find no way of explaining to the madman that although his village falls in Pakistan, as a non-Muslim he himself has to go to India. At last, in exasperation, Bishan Singh plants himself on a furrow in no-man's land and declares it to be his village. There he dies. Manto himself was a Bombayite of the Bohemian 1930s, whose partition stories have become paradigmatic for us in South Asia. There is, however, a curious point of departure in his work, from the quintessentially urban prepartition stories to the universalist stories he wrote during partition. It was not until I read an account of the 1947 riots in Bombay by the filmmaker Khwaja Ahmed Abbas, that I heard the same anguished mourn for the loss of a city that we had experienced in Delhi. And then the close similarity of the two laments started the uncomfortable thought: if he in 1947 spoke in the same voice as I in 1984, how rooted had the Delhi in my mind ever been or the Bombay in his?

In the years that followed the 1984 riots, communal wars — between Hindus and Muslims and Hindus and Sikhs in such cities as Delhi, Bombay, Hyderabad, Ahmedabad, and Surat — snapped the fragile city identities which so many of us had taken for granted, as marking the distinct urban cultures that our different regions had produced. Already these had subtly eroded, but in a countermovement to the communal rise which pushed us into collective enmities. By the 1980s, our groups could no longer be described as Delhiites, Hyderabadis, or Bombayites, but were an amalgam of transients from most of India's major cities — journalists and academics, artists and playwrights, and a range of activists from all over India. We had the freemasonry of a generation, but our childhoods, families, rituals, and practices had little in common. We were not only of different religions and castes and regions and mother tongues, but often of very different classes. For me this was the turning point at which I began to become cosmopolitan, despite my years at university in England. There I had acquired a none-too-pleasant familiarity with a culture whose literature had influenced me since childhood; here I became familiar with cultures and mores whose range had passed my enclave by.

These two trends of the 1980s, a rise in communal and nationalist violence and a sharp increase in the mobility of intellectuals, artists, and activists, were accompanied by a new exploration of collective and individual identities, a kind of mosaic-building of selves that excavated the secrets and lies of our families and our cities, and focused on moments of change and transfixion. While the exploration was most marked in the cinema, with a spate of both low-budget and popular films examining the interstices of community, minority, and individual relationships, there were similar explorations in painting, theater, and dance — the most notable of which interpreted famous women, both real and imaginary. Oddly enough, a parallel exploration was taking place among Indians in England, the United States, South Africa, and the West Indies. Third- and fourth-generation children of migrants from India, Pakistan, and Bangladesh, and of twice-migrant Indians from Uganda and Tanzania, began to ask what it was to be British, American, South African, or West Indies Indians. The question landed them in revolt on two separate fronts: in Britain, for example, a group like Southall Black Sisters found itself battling both English chauvinism and orthodox Indian reaction.

As Indian women in Southall and Bradford, Lenasia and Durban, New Jersey and Trinidad went public, we in India were made both painfully and pleasurably aware that we belonged to a much wider community than that in our subcontinent. We learned, too, that there was no simple distinction between Indian diasporas across the oceans and the diasporic sentiments which we carried within ourselves. In other words, an Ahmedabadi Muslim from Gujarat might find he had as much in common with a South African Gujarati Muslim as with a Hindu from Ahmedabad; a Sikh woman from Delhi might find she had as much in common with a Sikh woman from Southall as with a Hindu or Muslim woman from Delhi. By the early 1990s, satellite television and electronic mail, low-cost travel and telephone lines, the Internet and the integration of markets had all begun to blur territorial bounds of identity. An Indian in Jerusalem could watch live parliamentary debates in Delhi. A small-town Indian could watch an Indian in London anchoring a world news program. Both might watch the new Indian bands in New Jersey. Indians writing in English could live in New York, Toronto, London, Bombay, or Calcutta, but what they produced was seen as part of one corpus; whether in the visual arts, music, or dance, pan-Indian themes and styles had emerged.

This year, the 50th anniversary of Indian independence, there has been considerable comment in the international media on the somber tone of celebrations in India. These observations have contrasted especially with the widespread attention the anniversary has received in other parts of world, most notably in the United States, where it has been marked by a festival of Indian music at Carnegie Hall, a special issue of *The New Yorker* devoted to Indian writing, and a series of exhibitions of which *Out of India: Contemporary Art of the South Asian Diaspora* is the latest. Nevertheless, India's soul-searching has a point. In a 50th anniversary poll conducted by the magazine *India Today*, some 85 percent of those questioned said they would like to be reborn Indian (a quintessentially Asian question). On the other hand, when asked whether they thought India would stay together, over 40 percent said no.

I, myself, am inclined to read these answers metaphorically rather than literally. India has seen an extraordinary proliferation of assertions of identity in recent years, many of them in contexts of violence and corruption. On the political plane alone, the last decade has seen the end of one-party dominance and the rise of regional, religious, and caste parties. In the past, Indians have navigated within and between identities with skill and even occasional playfulness. A prime example of this was given by an eighteen-year-old called Rani. Rani came from a village near the central Indian city of Bhopal; she had, she told me, long been a rebel. When she was fifteen she started smoking; at seventeen she and her boyfriend stole Rs.1000 (about $25) from her parents and ran off to Bombay. For three days they had a wonderful time; then the money ran out. A simple story, but as Rani told it she tried out different voices and styles of telling. If one did not fit, she discarded it for another. In the end, I had a montage of Ranis, some in the grainy black and white of Bombay talkies, others with the smell of the cowbyre she said her parents had locked her in.

The trials of identity which we are currently undergoing, however, are different. While some of them may be ill-fitting, few are being tried out in play. Indeed, the range and depth with which identities are being explored by Indians today in literature and the visual arts is a revelation. It shows, to adapt Salman Rushdie's phrase, that India is again being sufficiently imagined. How various terms in which it is imagined will meld is unclear. For now, I am merely happy to see this new flowering. Like the Tamil at the concert, if you ask, "Enjoying?" my answer is, "Simply!"

RADHA KUMAR, Ph.D., is a 1996-97 Warren Weaver Fellow at the Rockefeller Foundation, whose publications include *A History of Doing: An Illustrated Account of Movements for Women's Rights and Feminism in India, 1800-1990* (Kali for Women and Verso Books, 1993), and *Bosnia-Herzegovina: Between War and Peace*, which she edited with Josep Palau (Generalitat Valencia, 1993).

A Brief History

by Jane Farver

At midnight on August 14, 1947, after one hundred and fifty years of struggle, India gained independence from Great Britain and two separate and sovereign nations — India and Pakistan — were born. The jubilation of the moment was captured by photographer Homai Vyarawalla, whose works are featured in the opening segment of this exhibition. However, as much as this event was a cause for rejoicing, new problems were being brought into existence. The boundaries drawn up between the new states did not necessarily take into account existing geographic, economic, or linguistic realities. Pakistan was divided not only from India, but was divided itself, occupying two parcels of land separated by 600 miles of hostile territory. In addition, West and East Pakistan had little in common with each other beyond a shared history of intense provincial particularism.

The political upheaval, communal violence, and displacement brought on by independence and partition resulted in nearly one million deaths, including that of Mohandas K. Gandhi, leader of the Indian nationalist movement, assassinated by a Hindu fanatic on January 30, 1948. Of the between 12 and 14 million rendered homeless by partition, about half were Hindu refugees who fled from Pakistan to India, and half were Muslims who made the journey the other way. Sikhs living in the riot-torn areas of central Punjab also were affected. When predominantly Muslim Kashmir was invaded by Pakistani-backed Pathan forces, its Hindu Maharaja opted for union with India, provoking the first India-Pakistan war. In 1949, a truce was brokered in Kashmir, and the area was divided along the cease-fire line with India holding about two-thirds of the territory and Pakistan the remainder.

India's first prime minister, Jawaharlal Nehru, guided the nation in adopting a new constitution in 1950, and remained in office until his death in 1964. However, in Pakistan, the death of Governor-General Mohammad Ali Jinnah just 13 months after independence led to political instability and a military coup by General Mohammad Ayub Khan in 1958. A little more than a decade later, disparity between East and West Pakistan, a second war with India in 1965 (again over Kashmir), and simmering unrest led to elections for a return to civilian rule. The 1970 election results ended in a political stalemate: Sheikh Mujibur Rahman's Awami League won a majority in the National Assembly by campaigning for autonomy for East Pakistan, while West Pakistan was carried by Zulifiqar Ali Bhutto.[1] These events precipitated an uprising in East Pakistan and a third war with India. In January 1972, East Pakistan was established as the independent state of Bangladesh with Sheikh Mujibur as prime minister.

As prime minster of India, Nehru followed a course of strict nonalignment in foreign affairs, and democratic socialism and secularism at home. He never shared Gandhi's vision of India as a "village republic," but believed India should become an industrialized nation. His policies resulted in a vast network of state-owned factories, and the "license raj," a system through which government officials determined products, prices, and markets for private enterprise.

When Nehru died, his successor, Lal Bahadur Shastri, survived him by only 19 months. Nehru's only child, Indira Gandhi, became prime minister in 1966. In 1971, Mrs. Gandhi won an overwhelming electoral victory, but she was soon accused of violating election laws — a charge upheld by a high court in June 1975. Mrs. Gandhi immediately declared a State of Emergency, postponing elections for two years, suspending civil liberties, and jailing political opponents without trial. Programs she put into effect during the Emergency — sweeping social reforms, economic planning, and forced birth control — proved controversial. Her Congress party was defeated by the Janata (People's) party, a coalition group headed by Morarji Desai in 1977. Gandhi was reelected in 1980, the same year her youngest son and closest advisor, Sanjay Gandhi, was killed in a plane crash.

The early 1980s were troubled times for Indira Gandhi: her cabinet and council of ministers resigned when the states of Andhra Pradesh and Karnataka, long controlled by the Congress party, were lost in the elections of 1983; massive demonstrations by Sikh nationalists pushing for autonomy took place in Punjab; and 3,000 died when Assamese Hindus rioted to prevent Muslim Bangladesh immigrants from voting. When radical Sikh youths attempting to win a separate Sikh state (Khalistan)[2] occupied the Golden Temple at Amritsar in 1984, Mrs. Gandhi launched "Operation Blue Star," sending Indian troops and tanks into the Temple grounds, killing many and seriously damaging one of India's most sacred monuments. Later that year, Indira Gandhi was assassinated by Sikh members of her own security force; and thousands of Sikhs were killed by Hindus in retaliatory violence throughout northern India. Her son Rajiv Gandhi was chosen as her successor.

The popular Rajiv Gandhi was believed to be free from corruption, but soon allegations of wrongdoing by his close associates, and his decisions to send troops to Sri Lanka and the Maldives, drew criticism. His efforts to quell violence by Sikhs and Kashmiri Muslims failed, and ethnic and tribal groups in the northeast, in Tamil Nadu, and in many other parts of India called for greater autonomy. Creating new ethnic states of

Nagaland and Mizoram and signing a peace accord with rebels in Tripura did not put an end to demands for more power in those areas. Fighting broke out in Assam between tribal groups and Bangladeshi migrants; and there was caste warfare in Andhra Pradesh and Bihar. In 1988, the Gurkhas gained local autonomy in Darjeeling. The ideal of a secularist, nationalist India was under siege from various communal, religious, and caste interests. The Congress party lost the 1989 elections, and Gandhi resigned. The National Front, led by V.P. Singh, formed a minority government; Singh was succeeded in 1990 by Chandra Shekar. Rajiv Gandhi ran for reelection in 1991, but was assassinated by a Tamil extremist during his campaign.

In 1991, P.V. Narasimha Rao of the Congress party became India's fourth prime minister in two years. Facing national bankruptcy, Rao discarded socialism for free markets, low tariffs, and foreign investments. In 1992, when Hindu extremists destroyed the Babari Masjid, a mosque in Ayodhya, the worst communal violence since independence erupted throughout India. Rao's party lost in 1996, but his successor, Hindu nationalist Bharatiya Janata party (BJP) leader Atal Bihari Vajpayee, resigned less than two weeks after taking office. United Front coalition candidate H.D. Deve Gowda, who replaced him, was himself replaced by the current prime minister, I.K. Gujral, in 1997.

The economic reforms begun under Narasimha Rao have produced a rapidly accelerated growth in the Indian middle class. New cars and apartment buildings, televisions, and cellular phones are commonplace in the cities where 26 percent of the population reside (a 50 percent increase since 1961). However, India remains agricultural and rural, and the majority of its people still reside in its more than 500,000 villages.[3] Since independence, changes have taken place in the villages including: paved roads, compulsory schooling for all children, irrigation for crops, and electricity to power television sets (although often for only a few hours a day). The population, which has almost tripled in its 50 years of independence, continues to grow by 13 million a year; and India, not China, is expected to be the world's most populous nation at some point in the 21st century. A nation of contrasts, India ranks among the top ten industrial nations in the world, but has one of the world's lowest per-capita incomes at U.S. $340 a year. Forty-eight percent of the population cannot read or write (64 percent of the men and 39 percent of the women) except for those living in Kerala, where a literacy rate of over 90 percent has been achieved. At the same time, India is one of the world's top producers of Ph.Ds.

Today, although many South Asian graduates of universities in England or the United States, who might once have emigrated, are returning to take advantage of job opportunities in India, there are still many Indians living in other parts of the world:

...there are major populations of Indian descent outside India, including over a million in Malaysia, Sri Lanka, and South Africa, nearly as many in both Great Britain and the United States; and about half a million each in Mauritius, Trinidad, Tobago, and Guyana, with smaller but significant numbers in the United Arab Emirates, Oman, Singapore, Yemen, and Suriname. There are, of course, tiny Indian minorities in a variety of countries, from some twenty thousand in Hong Kong to a solitary couple in El Salvador — and (until his premature death in 1994) one lone Indian, Bezal Jesudason, on the last outpost before the North Pole, running a base camp and provision store for Arctic explorers in the wilds of the aptly named and remote Canadian settlement of Resolute. In a statement in Parliament in May 1988, the government of India estimated that there were some 10 million Indians living in 155 countries around the world, including eight in Iceland, four in Kampuchea, and one in the Pacific island state of Vanuatu. But the government's figures conflated Indian passport-holders with known ethnic minorities of Indian descent, and its total of 10 million, though not an unreasonable guesstimate, cannot be arrived at by adding up the officially available statistics.[4]

Sikh farmers were the first to emigrate to the United States and Canada in the 1890s, settling in British Columbia and California. Anti-Indian riots occurred in the state of Washington in 1907 and, in 1914, 400 Sikhs aboard the Japanese ship *Komagata Maru* were denied entry into Vancouver and had to return to Bengal after almost a year at sea. In 1917, a court ruling barred immigrants from Asiatic countries from entering the United States. In 1926, the United States citizenship of 46 Indians was revoked by a ruling which was not rescinded until 1946, when it was decided that Indians could become citizens and enter the country on a limited quota. The McCarran-Walter Act of 1952 changed the base of the quotas to one of racial characteristics, placing Western Hemisphere and East African Indians together with East Indians in the same small quota. Until 1947, those South Asians who were able to come to the United States were mostly students. Their numbers increased somewhat after independence, and many students stayed on to command good salaries in science, engineering, and other fields. The Hart-Celler Immigration Act of 1965 finally dispensed with racial and country-of-origin quotas, and issued visas on the basis of familial relationships and occupational skills.[5] Significant numbers of working-class South

Asians began to arrive in the United States in the late 1970s and early 1980s, bringing their families with them. The number of Indians living in the United States is estimated to be one million, while there are 306,000 from Pakistan and 144,000 from Bangladesh. However, this number does not include illegal immigrants, or those who came to the United States from Trinidad, Tobago, Guyana, or nations other than India.

When the East India Company gained control of parts of India in the 18th century, Indians began coming to Britain as seamen or employees of ex-colonial families. By the late 19th century, sons of upper- and middle-class Indians were sent to study in Britain, and India's future leaders, Gandhi, Nehru, and Jinnah, would emerge from this group. By the 1920s and 1930s, there was a settled Indian population in Britain, which grew rapidly during the postwar years. The first group to come were some 30,000 Eurasians of mixed European and Indian heritage who identified closely with Britain and chose to leave India after independence. Working-class South Asians began to emigrate to Britain in the 1950s to fill jobs created by a postwar economic boom; and the 1970s saw an influx of Indians who had been expelled from East Africa after some African states gained independence, including 28,000 driven out of Uganda by General Idi Amin in 1972. Today approximately 1,450,000 people from India, Pakistan, Bangladesh, and Sri Lanka live in Britain.[6]

Endnotes

1. Under Bhutto, Pakistan devised a new constitution in 1973 which Bhutto failed to fully implement. Accusations of vote-rigging by opposition groups and outbreaks of violence provided another pretext for a military coup led by General Mohammad Zia-ul Haq. When Zia became president the following year, he banned all political parties; and Bhutto was imprisoned and executed on murder charges in 1979. Zia attempted to give legitimacy and popularity to his government by emphasizing the Islamic nature of Pakistani society. He remained in power until 1985, when he lifted martial law and held elections for civilian rule. Zia was elected and stayed in office until 1988 when his military-political alliance broke down. He dismissed his cabinet, dissolved the national and provincial assemblies, and announced new elections which took place in spite of Zia's death in a plane crash. The Pakistan People's party won and the premiership went to Benazir Bhutto, daughter of Zulifiqar Ali Bhutto. She was ousted in 1996 on charges of corruption and extrajudicial killings in Karachi. Mohammad Nawaz Sharif was elected Prime Minister in February 1997.

2. They were led by Sikh fundamentalist preacher Jarnail Singh Bhindrwale whom Indira Gandhi had formerly backed for partisan purposes.

3. Shashi Tharoor, *India: From Midnight to the Millennium* (New York: Arcade, 1997), 105.

4. Tharoor, 146-47.

5. Mark Leeds, *Ethnic New York* (Lincolnwood, Illinois: Passport Books, 1995), 470.

6. Ian McAuley, *Ethnic London* (Lincolnwood, Illinois: Passport Books, 1995), 25-26.

Inside and Out of India: Contemporary Art of the South Asian Diaspora

by Jane Farver

Out of India: Contemporary Art of the South Asian Diaspora brings artists from what was colonial India together with artists of South Asian descent from other parts of the world, including Britain, the United States, Thailand, and Canada. In tribute to the 50th anniversary of the independence of India and the creation of Pakistan, this exhibition begins with a selection of works by **Homai Vyarawalla**, India's first and, for some time, only professional woman photographer.

When she was born into a priestly Parsi family in Navsari-Gujarat in 1913, Homai's birth horoscope predicted she would roam with royalty. Encouraged by her future husband, Vyarawalla took up freelance photography while attending Sir J.J. School of Art in Bombay. As a husband and wife team they did photo features and covered wartime activities for the *Illustrated Weekly of India* and the Far Eastern Bureau of the British Information Service in Delhi. Carrying her equipment with her on a bicycle, Vyarawalla photographed everything from fancy-dress parties at the Delhi Gymhkana to the first Independence Day address at the Red Fort, and everyone from Gandhi, Nehru, Jinnah, and the Mountbattens to Queen Elizabeth and Ho Chi Minh. Her camera captured the intense optimism of the early years of the nation as well. However, by the early 1970s, Vyarawalla had stopped working altogether, depressed by a new breed of politicians and by security systems that prevented her from photographing individuals and events as she wished.

Vyarawalla and other photographers working in the early years of the Indian nation were consciously engaged in constructing the image of the nation. From their photos emerged

> ...the visage of the politician as the romantic hero of the times — a dreamer and a visionary — the Nehrus and the Gandhis and a whole band of 'nationalist' politicians who appear before the camera with disarming candor and geniality. It is a sort of image construction which the hermeneutics of that time 'permits,' enabling us an easy entry into a nation in formation. And it is precisely such a visual formation the present resists, despite the far more accomplished penetrative powers of present day camera technology. What her Rolliflex lacked in terms of technological sophistication is abundantly compensated for by the fact that she is as much a recorder of events as an accomplice in them.[1]

Vyarawalla's work, which went unremembered for many years, was "rediscovered" in 1986 by photographer **Satish Sharma**, whose work offers a marked contrast to hers. Sharma makes portraits of political leaders not from Vyarawalla's insider position, but by photographing the effigies, posters, and other surrogate images India's politicians now offer the public in place of themselves.

Postwar painters, sculptors, and printmakers in India were also involved in the creation of a national image, and they were attracted to Modernism because it represented progress and change for India. In the words of Geeta Kapur, the artist aspired to become a central national figure — a concept based upon a myth of lost communities, nationalism, and modern utopian idealism. Modernity went largely unquestioned, or if it were it was on the basis of a constructed, secularized tradition invented in the name of nationalism. In recent years, however, Indian artists have begun to interrogate the past. As Kapur states:

> In so doing, we recognized in hindsight a certain bad faith in some of the terms of nationalist cultural discourse. In particular, the sectarian and religious was not looked at directly but was often smuggled in, making both the modern and the secular into well-meaning but too quickly exposed masquerades....What most needed questioning in recent decades was the artist's presumed expertise in slicing through the layers of this stratified society, as if to touch simultaneously the high caste, the *dalit* (a person of low caste, an untouchable), and the tribal cultures — to draw from them imaginative inspiration but to leave the source compressed within a too steeply hierarchical structure. What also needed to be challenged in the postindependence period was the mapping of the artistic imaginary onto a transcendent horizon, for this was the scale at which the heroic self-representation of the national artist was pitched.[2]

Most of the artists in this exhibition have had no direct experience of colonialism, and early postcolonial debates over indigenism and the creation of a national identity, a nativist aesthetic, or a self-consciously "modern" Indian culture mean little to them. As Ranjit Hoskote has said of such artists:

> As the momentum of nationalist sentiment has waned and our prior concept of the nation-state has fallen into discredit, the pressure on the artist to participate in the national drama has been greatly diminished. [They] are able to side-step the demands made on them by a conscriptive notion of citizenship and indeed, have subjected that notion to critique.[3]

These artists seem to be responding to *denationalized* condition, a term I have borrowed from Sau-Ling C. Wong's essay, "Denationalization Reconsidered: Asian American Cultural Criticism at a Theoretical Crossroads."[4] He identifies three main factors that contribute to this denationalized state. Wong is speaking specifically of Asian Americans, but his thoughts can be applied to South Asian and British artists as well. First is what Wong calls "the easing of cultural nationalist concerns" due to changing demographics in the Asian American population and the influx of theoretical critiques from various quarters ranging from the poststructuralist to the gay and lesbian. He sees the easing of cultural nationalism (which was committed to an aggressively masculine agenda) as the growing acceptance by Asian Americans of Asian influences (which were formerly often identified as feminine) once disavowed out of fear of exoticization.

The second factor Wong cites is the increasing permeability in the boundaries between Asian Americans and 'Asian Asians' brought on by the economic and political positions now being assumed by Asia and America. As capital becomes increasingly transnational, borders become lesser obstacles, and workers migrate the world. E-mail, fax, inexpensive jet travel, and less costly international telephone rates have greatly increased communication and travel back and forth between South Asia and Europe or North America, at least for those of a certain socioeconomic class. Information from around the world can be accessed globally and instantaneously via the Internet; newspapers are available in many languages; the latest H/Bollywood productions can be rented at the video store; and the latest music, books, and art magazines are also attainable. Immigration is not the one-sided attempt at assimilation it once was; nor is it any longer possible to avoid outside influences by staying "home." However, as Wong states, increased penetration of cultural borders can, paradoxically, have other consequences, such as the worldwide rise of various forms of fundamentalism that insist on absolute purity and inviolate borders.

The third is a shift from a domestic perspective focusing on Asian Americans as an ethnic/racial minority within the national boundaries of the United States to a diasporic perspective that views Asian Americans as but one segment of a global dispersal of people of Asian origin. Only a diasporic perspective can accommodate complex backgrounds like those of some artists in this exhibition, who were born or lived in places such as Africa or the Caribbean before migrating to Britain or the United States. Possessing a kind of double vision, they insist upon their right to multiple subjectivities; and their cultural identity is not constricted by geography.

Geeta Kapur may be speaking of the easing of cultural nationalism when she asks, "What was the norm that needed to be dismantled in Indian art? I would answer that there was a properly clad, national/modern that was by and large male. And it may be that it is being stripped bare by the brides, even!" [5] Kapur is pointing out the role women artists have had in recent years in de/reconstructing the identity of the Indian artist, citing artists such as **Nalini Malani**, whose paintings, performances, and films address the effects of neocolonialism. Malani's watercolors in this exhibition are about mutilation, betrayal, and control; they point to a fractured social contract and bad faith. Her timeless figures defy specific classification and speak to any and/or all cultures on the roles of women and men, those discriminated against, and the underprivileged. Two of Malani's works in this exhibition are related to *Heiner Mueller's Medea*, a large collaborative project she did with Alaknanda Samarth in Mumbai (Bombay) in 1994. Malani has written about this work:

> …the nexus between the alchemist princess Medea — who was marginalized as a barbarian in Corinth — and Jason the colonizer, was a metaphor for the Third World and the First World — a nexus that preoccupies me a great deal…it was a sadomasochistic relationship that could only lead to death and genocide. Intolerance, degradation and projecting the bad into the other are the makings of a fascist society. We experienced strong shades of this with the Bombay riots in the winter of 1992. [6]

The Bombay riots Malani refers to took place after an event which shook India to its core: the destruction by Hindus of the Babari Masjid in Ayodhya, Uttar Pradesh.[7] For many artists inside and outside of India this event was a signal call that the old secular ideal was endangered.

New York artist **Vijay Kumar** was a child of partition who had to leave his birthplace of Lahore and move with his family to Lucknow, a city close to Ayodhya in Uttar Pradesh. He describes Lucknow as a beautiful city known for its polite language and gentle manners which taught him people of different backgrounds could live with tolerance and respect for each other. When Kumar read the December 7, 1992, *New York Times* article about the razing of the mosque, he immediately was moved to make work about it. That article and subsequent others became the grounds for his *India Portfolio*, a series of 18 intaglios and photoetchings. Over photoetchings of the articles Kumar superimposed a second plate of his own drawings, and they, as well as a sense of his outrage and despair, seem to emerge directly out of the printed words.

New Delhi artist **Vivan Sundaram's** *HOUSE* also was created in response to the communal violence surrounding Ayodhya. This work, part painting, part architecture, has walls of white handmade paper, a rusted steel skeleton, and a fragile glass ceiling. Shapes of hand tools and common objects — a shovel, a saw, a paper window — are embossed on two walls, and the third is covered with the artist's vigorous markings and the outline of a hand. On the fourth wall, delicate stains trace the rusting of industrial materials onto the paper. Inside, a small steel bench is placed next to a bowl filled with water, beneath which glimmers a video image of fire. Are we looking at a hearth fire or a house on fire?

In Indian villages, one can now see at night the flickering blue light of a television screen emanating even from the doors and windows of houses as small as this one. (40 million of the population of 950 million now own televisions). Some suggest that television is contributing to communal tensions not only by making poorer Indians aware of the widening gap between themselves and the rich,[8] but also by fueling nationalist fervor through religious programs:

> ...the new discovery is the dramatization of religious tales. A major event in the history of Indian television was undoubtedly the broadcasting of the *Ramayana* in the form of a serial rivaling the length of "Dallas" or "Dynasty," starting in January, 1987. This has done more than anything else to make a standard version of the epic known and popular among the Indian middle class. Moreover, it greatly enhanced the general public's knowledge of Ayodhya as Rama's birthplace and therefore as one of the most important places of pilgrimage in Uttar Pradesh. In this way the controversy concerning the mosque built "on Rama's birthplace" has become an issue that is highly loaded with affect in the popular imagination."[9]

Sundaram's India is a contemporary one, where old traditions and new influences constantly jar intrudingly upon each other, and he refuses to find comfort in either. His is an India in a state of social trauma brought on by what author Nigel Harris calls:

> ...integration in the world economy via what is called liberalization — the stage and style of capitalism which the IMF and the World Bank dictate to the developing world. This is an internationalism under duress in that its first condition is the delinking of growth from any form of nationalism but precisely through the diabolic inversion of the needs of manoeuvre between the first and third worlds....
> Institutionally, the old socialized state, the embodiment of the social contract, is also being reordered. It had for so long been the dominant partner in the national alliance that its withdrawal in favour of private interests — those supposedly integrated into world markets — is continuing to cause social shocks. Furthermore, world markets seem to demand such a degree of flexibility on the part of national economies in response to external changes, that the old structures produced by the political will of the social contract are no longer defensible — the large public sectors directed along political rather than economic lines, welfare, health, education and housing programmes, and so on.[10]

The city of Bombay permeates **Atul Dodiya's** paintings. His *Sunday Morning, Marine Drive* is a view of Bombay's Back Bay from Marine Drive toward Malabar Hill, the expensive residential area visible across the bay. Strolling pedestrians, a cow (sacred to Hindus), a man sleeping on the median strip, and a deformed beggar share the painting space with several images of the painter, including ghostly outlines of the figures of two men — one urinating into the bay, and one using nose drops — that refer to the pollution of the city and its waters. The painting, which depicts the city's most popular promenade should, perhaps, be retitled. Bombay is headquarters of the Shiv Sena, a militant Hindu political party whose numbers are growing at a rapid pace, even attracting members from the lower ranks of the city's police force. The Shiv Sena-led government in Maharashtra has given new names to the city and many of its streets and landmarks. Bombay is now called by its Marathi name Mumbai, while Marine Drive is now called Netaji Subhashchandra Bose Road.[11]

Dodiya's *2nd October* depicts Mumbai, recognizable by the distinctive tower in the background, on Gandhi's birthday. The statue of Gandhi is being garlanded by a solitary worker in a giant crane; and the painting's surface appears torn and ruptured and in the same state of decrepitude as parts of the city itself. Dodiya asks whether Mumbai, Gandhi's home from 1917 to 1934 and the city where he launched his *satyagrahas* (civil disobedience movements), was arrested, and sent to prison, might not owe more to his legacy than perfunctory obeisance in the form of official garlands of flowers.

Mumbai was one of the cities hardest hit in the aftermath of Ayodhya when violent episodes took place immediately after the mosque was destroyed and exactly one month later. Over 1,000 people in the city were killed — the majority of them Muslims. The killings were instigated and carried out in Mumbai by the Shiv Sena, which, although banned, was, according to a number of reports in English-language news media, actively supported by Mumbai police.[12] Violence erupted again in Mumbai on March 12, 1993, when 13 bombs were detonated throughout the city, killing 250. The stock exchange, the Air India building, three of the top-rated hotels near the airport, and other commercial establishments were destroyed. Although no one claimed responsibility for the bombings, many Indian politicians blamed Pakistan for planting the bombs as punishment for the many Muslims killed in the riots. One hundred eighty-nine people were arrested in connection with the bombings, but the cases have not yet been solved.

"Hand Me Your Keys" is Atul Dodiya's depiction of the thousand-armed demon goddess Durga, an incarnation of Shiva's consort Parvati. In Dodiya's painting, Durga assumes the form of a metal detector, ubiquitous in Mumbai after the bombings. Body parts — appropriated from Picasso's *Guernica* — are scattered throughout the work, and the attributes of the many-armed goddess surround the metal detector. In the works in this exhibition Dodiya is commenting on the effects of modernity and technology on India.

The introduction of technology into India is also of interest to **Ayisha Abraham**, whose series of computer-manipulated colonial photographs, *...looks the other way*, considers the role of the camera in the invention of identity as well as the history of religious conversion in India.

Abraham's father came from the Syrian Christian community while her mother's family was upper-caste Hindus converted to Protestantism by Scottish Presbyterian missionaries in the 19th century.[13] Such conversions were rare because they resulted in the loss of caste status. Photos from her mother's family, which prompted Abraham to investigate the concept of conversion, were also the source for *...looks the other way*. This title refers to a 1925 photo taken in Madras of a group of Indians and whites (missionaries?) posing for the camera. As the others stare into the camera, one Western woman is looking at something off in the distance, disrupting the hierarchical colonial image. Abraham has stated, "...'look' and 'other' seem to imply the historical linking together of techniques of seeing and of vision with that of studying and looking at the 'Other', racially, culturally, etc...."[14]

Using computer-manipulated imagery which is (re)producible without a negative, Abraham questions the "photographic truth" of the colonial images. By converting them — by making subtle changes or focusing on small, seemingly unimportant details in them — she is able to give a different visual account of empire and to elucidate the roles women played in both colonial and national patriarchal cultures.

Issues of caste also occupy the works of **N.N. Rimzon** and **Ravinder G. Reddy**, particularly in relation to the many who were outside of the Hindu caste system, which in addition to Muslims and Christians included Untouchables, called *Harijans* or Children of God by Gandhi, and also known as the scheduled castes or *Dalits*.[15] The Dalits, who were not allowed to live near or even be seen by caste members, took care of corpses and worked in trades such as tanning or shoemaking. They were not allowed to drink from the same water sources as the upper

castes, nor were they permitted to enter temples lest they pollute those who came into contact with them. Untouchableness was formally abolished in 1950 by the Indian constitution which also reserves admissions to universities, a percentage of government jobs, and a number of Parliament seats for scheduled castes as remediation. The caste system's hold on educated urban India is slipping, but the practice continues on many levels, particularly in rural areas:

> Despite fifty years of freedom, well-trained and enlightened administrators, and politically correct rhetoric at all levels, caste continues to enslave village society. Each week brings a new horror story into the national press. A Dalit woman is stripped and paraded naked through the streets of her village because her son dared to steal from an upper-caste Thakur....In one village twenty-two "uppity" Untouchables are gunned down in an upper-caste massacre; in another, four hundred Dalit families are burned out of their huts for daring to demand the legal minimum wage for their labors. These are not isolated incidents, in that dozens like them are reported every year. But on the other hand they are not cause for despair about the prospects of social change in rural India. Indeed they are evidence of resistance to change rather than of the impossibility of it. The victims of these crimes had dared to challenge the proscriptions of the traditionalists; they had tried to lift the dead weight of the ages off their backs. [16]

Trivandrum-based N.N. Rimzon often uses certain traditional Indian symbols, such as the Tirthankara Jain figure or the sword, to reflect the tensions of a multifaceted India where regional, national, and increasingly international influences are at odds. *Faraway from One Hundred and Eight Feet*, included in this exhibition, is comprised of 108 (a multiple of nine and an auspicious number in Hindu rituals) identical terra-cotta pots with a handmade broom and a length of rope protruding from each. Rimzon's pots snake like a spinal cord in a long sinewy line on the ground. *Faraway from One Hundred and Eight Feet* refers to a time when entrance to the city of Poona (now Pune) was denied to any Untouchable who was not wearing a pot (suspended from the neck) and a broom (attached at the leg). The pot was to catch any of their spittle that might pollute the ground, and the broom was to wipe out all traces of their footsteps.

Unglazed terra-cotta pots like those in Rimzon's piece have been made in India's villages in a continuing tradition for over 4,000 years; and the craft of its more than one million potters has been little affected by the modern world. Since prehistoric times, the vessel has been regarded as a symbol of the mother goddess and used for secular and religious functions. The potter generally provides for the needs of his local vicinity, using clay that comes from the earth nearby. His wares return to the earth when broken or no longer needed in an endless recycling of its resources. Rimzon's use of repetition in *Faraway from One Hundred and Eight Feet* is evocative of this ongoing tradition of human labor, as well as a sense of connection to the Indian soil.

Beneath their sensuous gilding and rich colors, Visakhapatnam artist Ravinder G. Reddy's iconic figures possess the features of the laboring class, the Dalits, and the tribal peoples. They betray a caste system that still determines purity by birth lines and Aryan features. Figures in his *Family*, quietly absorbed in daily tasks are, by being naked and colored Krishna's blue, removed from the world of the profane to that of the sacred. Reddy's monumental *Krishna Veni*[17] elevates one of India's village women to a state of divinity. As he reclaims status for those he depicts in his sculptures, Reddy also reclaims the right to continue and extend one of the greatest sculptural traditions the world has known. With humor, he transforms classical Indian sculpture into popular fetish objects, recognizing and retaining the eroticism of the earlier tradition in the contemporary one.

Sau-Ling C. Wong made the point that cultural nationalist concerns had eased due to the influx of critiques from various quarters.[18] As many artists, formerly silent or invisible in the South Asian community, began to press for their concerns to be recognized and acknowledged, they made possible multiple subjectivities within South Asian identity.

Nasreen Mohamedi was, like Nalini Malani, one of the women artists in India who helped to "dismantle the norm in Indian art." Born in Karachi, she moved to Bombay in 1944, was educated in London and Paris, taught in Baroda, and died in Kihim in India in 1990. Geeta Kapur has said of her:

> I want to make the proposition that Nasreen's work is about the self and body through a series of displacements, and that those insistently elided questions offer up the meaning of her work. That therefore she is within a great lineage of abstraction in a way that no other Indian artist is and that also she is without the tradition being a woman artist working in India at a time when there were few others of her kind.[19]

Mohamedi's abstraction offered an alternative to the productions of the male-dominated world of Indian figurative painting. She created painstakingly ruled drawings which like works of Agnes Martin or Carl Andre employed the grid. However, Mohamedi favored a more intuitive and poetic sense of geometry, and her grid was never absolute. The source of her work was to be

found in Islamic architecture, or in the photographs that she took, but chose not to exhibit, of a street in the rain, waves on a beach, or the paved courtyard at Fatehpur Sikri. From these she abstracted the sense of a body in space, of light and shadow, of sound and time. Her drawings are all the more remarkable for their control and precision in that Mohamedi suffered from a debilitating physical condition.

Sunil Gupta was born in India, holds Canadian citizenship, and resides in Britain. As an active curator and critic, Gupta has been at the forefront of efforts to bring the black arts movement (which in Britain includes artists of Caribbean, South Asian, and Middle Eastern heritage as well as African) to the attention of a wider public. In his *TRESPASS 3* series, Gupta has been working with specific sites, "reinserting" historical evidence no longer obviously present back into the landscape. He records this evidence in the form of computer-generated iris prints composed of juxtaposed disparate images.

TRESPASS 3, which Gupta produced as part of his fellowship in photography at Essex University, places the landscape surrounding Essex in a new context. Although the ports of Essex once did a thriving business in the slave trade, no physical traces of that history remain. Gupta's seemingly unconnected images reveal the trade and migrant history that Essex shares with non-European countries. His images forge psychic links between visible commercial, industrial, or tourist enterprises and the unseen individuals who labored in connection with them.

Samena Rana (1955-1992) was brought to the United Kingdom from Pakistan to receive medical treatment for an injury she received at age nine. Rana spent the remainder of her life in Britain, and in a wheelchair. As a photographer Rana explored the double issues of identity and disability; and as an activist she advocated greater accessibility to photo studios, darkroom facilities, colleges, and galleries. She fought to open up the male- and able-bodied-dominated profession of photography to the disabled.

Rana's strong, sensuous images project an atmosphere of danger. Fabrics and jewelry in deep, rich colors and textures mix with shards of glass or mirrors, the gleaming edge of a knife blade, and/or images of herself and her wheelchair. Rana has written about her work:

> The images encompass my past, present, and future.... Through the layers of water, diffused colours and a series of metaphors, I reconstruct my feelings which are about loss, trials and reclamation. There is a great sense of confusion and vagueness about myself and about my identity in the latter

images. Especially when I first became (dis)abled and came to England, a sense of isolation, displacement and fragmentation prevails. Harmony and integration come and go and the broken pieces do become cohesive, even the grey metallic wheelchair merges itself with the more sensual aspect of myself. Aesthetically womanhood and (dis)ability become integral to each other. [20]

Poulomi Desai, **Permindar Kaur**, and **Chila Kumari Burman** are all children of immigrant parents. Such individuals often have a special way of coping with their bicultural situation, which author Sonali Fernando describes in the following way:

> …For the children of migrants, however, knowledge of their parents' cultural codes is usually partial or derivative. Their skill is in moving laterally from one cultural code to another, they produce meaning synchronically (by simultaneous association) as much as diachronically (by history or code). This is an associative practice, a way of working dynamically and honestly with partial cultural memory and diverse contemporary experience, rather than a linear practice that seeks to excavate or reinforce tradition. It requires a different kind of intuition. What happens is a kind of "doubling" of vision, though not one that entails dualism. [21]

London artist Poulomi Desai's color inkjet prints, *Shakti Queens,* offer a glimpse into an often hidden lifestyle. Her South Asian transvestite subjects are beautiful, vulnerable, and engagingly open to her camera. Furthermore, they have stars in their eyes — Hindi film stars, to be exact. Desai is interrogating Britain's exoticization of India, but her manipulated images raise further issues of identity and sexuality, and lead viewers to question their own preconceptions.

Desai has stated that much of her work is intrinsically classified as South Asian or about women, but is not a direct response and she doesn't feel she has to be a positive role model. This attitude is a distinguishing mark of artists of younger generations. As more South Asian artists emerge in Britain, North America, and elsewhere, and there are more exhibitions, catalogues, and critical evaluations of the work of South Asian artists, the pressure for artists to represent anyone beside themselves is lessened. Permindar Kaur, a British artist of Sikh origin, has stated that she no longer feels there is a direct polarization between two distinct cultures in her work. While her work may still contain questions of identity, or contain references to a different religious or historical life, her work is directly related to the personal. Kaur makes objects that have their sources in domestic settings or childhood — beds, cots, chairs, dolls, and dolls' clothing. However, something in their scale or demeanor makes it

impossible for the viewer to obtain comfort from them. Because of her Sikh origins, there is always the temptation to read the works as coming from a diasporic sense of dislocation and loss. But, this is by no means the only possible reading of her work. Kaur's polar fleece dolls are limp and faceless, and they assume postures that speak of unhealthy relationships. Like dolls a therapist might use to interrogate an abused child, the 76 dolls in *You and Me,* included in this exhibition, stand in for us and allow us to project our histories onto them.

Chila Kumari Burman is the daughter of a Hindu-Punjabi family that emigrated to Britain in the 1950s and settled in Liverpool. Burman was one of the first South Asian British women to study at an art school and produce art of a political nature. Lacking a support structure when she was a beginning artist, she has worked to create one for others by curating exhibitions, writing criticism, and participating in many residencies in schools and colleges.

Burman refuses to be constricted to any traditional or expected image of a South Asian woman. She has instead created multiple identities for herself, including: the goddess Kali; the Rani of Jhansi, who fought the British during what was called the Mutiny of 1857; Phooli Devi, who sought to avenge the Untouchables; Hindi screen goddess Meena Kumari; and the "Wild Woman between Two Cultures," an expert at the Japanese martial art of Shotokan. These alter egos appear in a dizzying array in *Fly Girl Watching the World*, a mixed media and laser print work in which both identity and medium are manipulated to form a seemingly endless range of possibilities.

Burman's other works in the exhibition are cibachrome prints based on family photos. To these photos — which depict her father's tiger-topped ice-cream van; her mother, grandmother, and the Queen; and Burman with her sister at Bootle Girls Grammar School — she has added color and superimposed imagery to heighten their narrative quality, as she utilizes the personal to address issues of community, ethnicity, and nation.

The increasing permeability in the boundaries between South Asian artists and South Asians living outside of the subcontinent can be seen in the works of a number of the artists in *Out of India*. Now residents of New York City and Houston, Texas, respectively, **Mariam Ishaque** and **Shahzia Sikander** are both from Pakistan. Each reclaims and contemporizes the tradition of Indian miniature painting in her work, but in different ways. Ishaque's delicate, almost monochromatic works emphasize the contrasting use of space in Western and Indian miniature painting traditions. In *Flat-Footed Traveler*, Ishaque sets up Western perspective in the landscape, then subverts it by inhabiting the space with identically sized horses, denying the woman in the composition any potential for movement or escape. *Bachelor's Travels I* traps the figure of a woman within a web of lines, defining a space that refers to Western abstraction. Ishaque's paintings consistently point to the immobility of women within certain social constructs.

Even while she was studying miniature painting at the National College of Arts in Lahore, Shahzia Sikander transgressed the rules of the medium of the miniature; she would change their format, depict herself in them, and violate their decorative borders. When she came to the United States to study at the Rhode Island School of Design, she retained the painstaking method of the miniature, burnishing handmade paper and making her own vegetable dyes. However, she transgressed further by inserting contemporary forms into the miniatures to create fantasies that combine art historical, mythological, religious, and personal imagery. Within the confines of the miniature, Sikander may add an area of pure abstraction, paint the veil of a Muslim woman over the Hindu image of Durga, or indulge in radical shifts in scale. By inventing a vocabulary of loosely painted forms that reflect her concerns as a woman and an artist, Sikander aims to "highlight some fundamental issues of resistance, misrepresentation, and cultural exploitation." [22]

Rina Banerjee, born in Calcutta, arrived in the United States from London at the age of seven in 1970 with the first influx of Indians on the East Coast. She grew up in LeFrak City, Queens. Banerjee's essentially abstract sculptures and installations evoke a presence that is sharply feminine. She combines alluring materials like silk sari cloth, brilliantly colored pigments, and incense in an exoticized mix with more unlikely materials, such as stuffing from an old couch, burnt-out light bulbs, pins, duct tape, and string. In some cases, furniture is used to allude to the body. Like Permindar Kaur's dolls, Banerjee's works have a surrogate quality, possible stand-ins for women who have violence and lunacy projected onto them daily.

Banerjee has the ability to invest the abstract with conceptual content and to make art of exceptional visual beauty out of unthinkable materials. Her hybrid works attract and repel but also always contain humor. Banerjee says, "The viewer is both pleasured by the exotic object and simultaneously perplexed by its assertion." [23] This same dynamic affects the hybridized immigrant who must deal with lingering colonialist and racist mechanisms on a daily basis.

Born in Dublin and raised in Trinidad, **Shani Mootoo** now resides in Vancouver, Canada. To locate herself as an emerging painter in a country with a strong regional landscape tradition, she incorporated henna and *mendhi* (bright Indian dyes) and photocopied images of herself into her works. Mootoo found she liked working with the photocopier because it was "a machine without a history"; and she used it to create a series of vibrant posters and prints. Plastering these on walls in imitation of those in urban areas, she created "Ad Walls" that attracted through their color and pattern, but which also contained messages that reflected her diasporic perspective. Like Chila Kumari Burman, Mootoo resists conforming to preconceived notions of identity, stating: "I'm so often turned into a specimen — a raced, queered, gendered, or nationed person. All those things are part of me, but when isolated, they change me from a complex person — like we all are — to fit a theory." [24] Mootoo, who also resists being limited to any single medium or discipline to express her ideas, has also worked in video and is a published author.

Allan deSouza was born of Indian parents in Nairobi, Kenya, raised in Britain, and lives in Los Angeles. For his series *Threshold*, deSouza has been "photographing waiting or in-transit space, places of arrival and departure, anticipation and release; spaces located physically within but often legally outside the national border." [25] Supposedly neutral, airports and train stations are, in fact, sites of power and anxiety for those hoping to cross borders into new lives. Presented in small format, these locations have the jewel-like beauty of Indian miniatures, but further examination reveals a desolation in them and possible danger. Travel of another kind is examined in deSouza's second series of small-format photographs. Statues of elephants and Mughal domes and minarets may speak of the Indian subcontinent, but they do so from sites in Portugal, the Taj Mahal Casino in Atlantic City, and Disneyland.

New Delhi photographer **Pablo Bartholomew** traveled throughout the United States to photograph his *Indians in America* series. He depicts Jains eating tacos in upstate New York; Sikh farm workers eating *parathas* for lunch in Yuba, California; and Indians riding on a float decorated with a mammoth American flag in New York City. More poignant images include a Sikh funeral in California and a Hindu marriage in Connecticut, both carried out in American vernacular-style edifices; and thousands of South Asians praying in front of the Unisphere in Flushing Meadows Corona Park. Through Bartholomew's lens we see the myriad ways Indian immigrants have learned to adapt this country to their cultural needs, and vice-versa.

Dayanita Singh's photographs of those she calls well-to-do, metro business people and their families provide us with a view of a lifestyle almost as hidden as that of Poulomi Desai's *Shakti Queens*. In the world of Indian photography and in photographs of India, where we have come to expect images of aching poverty, exotic spirituality, or landscapes of beauty and terror, images like Singh's are rare. Her subjects have leisure time, money, servants, and pets. Singh's insider's view of the lifestyle of her friends, families, and acquaintances, a kind of lifestyle generally thought to exist only in Western cities, offers one of the only truly alternative views of contemporary life in India.

A number of the artists in this exhibition possess the complex backgrounds that only a diasporic perspective can accommodate. **Zarina** was a child of partition whose family and friends were among the millions who left their homes to seek shelter and safety elsewhere. When the circumstances of her later life demanded that she move often and create homes in many cities, she came to understand that home is not a permanent place but a concept we carry within us. That idea took the form of a house-on-wheels, and it has become a central image in her work. One of Zarina's works, included in this exhibition, incorporates thousands of tiny peripatetic house/wagons made of painted cast aluminum embarked on a nomadic journey. This work's title is taken from a line from the Urdu poem, *Morning of Independence*, written in 1947 by Faiz Ahmed Faiz, that reads, "Somewhere the flotilla of sorrow will come to rest." *Homes I Made/A Life in Nine Lines*, also included, is a portfolio of nine etchings with chine collé. Each print depicts the floor plan of a house Zarina has lived in since leaving India in 1958. Beginning with Bangkok and ending with New York, the series also includes New Delhi, Paris, Bonn, Tokyo, Los Angeles, and Santa Cruz.

Mohini Chandra traveled to the United States, Canada, New Zealand, Australia, and Fiji to research her family's history. Her ancestors were indentured servants who left India to work in Fiji, a community that has experienced a second diaspora due to recent political, cultural, and economic pressures.[26] *Album Pacific* is an installation of the backs of photos Chandra collected from albums and wallets along the way. The photos are hung in a complex map delineating her family trees and the journeys the photos and their owners have made since early in the century. As the fronts of the photos are not visible, we are left to decipher those diasporic journeys and relationships through the wear and tear and markings and inscriptions on the reverse. We deduce the stories of Chandra's subjects in the same fragmented and cryptic way that many diasporic individuals learn their own histories.

In **Shaheen Merali's** installation, *Going Native*, the viewer is invited to rest in pristine white canvas deck chairs, to watch a videotape of Franciscan monks gathering and dispersing on an otherwise deserted Goan beach, and to listen to a soundtrack of samples of Goan, Indian, and Western music, mixed with the sound of breathing and lapping waves. [27] Slides of tourists relaxing and engaging in various activities at Goan swimming pools and beaches are projected onto the viewer and the deck chairs.

Goa, one of the most beautiful parts of India, has seen multiple occupations throughout its history, from the arrival of the Portuguese in 1510, followed by the Jesuit missionaries led by St. Francis Xavier in 1542, to those still following the "hippie trail" that leads to Goa's beaches today. For Merali, a British artist of Indian heritage born in Dar es Salaam, Tanzania, a visit to Goa is loaded with implications of doubled colonialisms. Portugal's Vasco da Gama was the first European to visit Tanzania, and the Portuguese conducted trade along the coast until 1698 when they were expelled by Arabs from Oman. The British took over the area, then called German East Africa after World War I, but many Indians were forced to leave when certain African states gained their independence. That Merali visits India as a British tourist, as well as a native once or twice removed, is reinforced by the slides projected onto the deck chairs, which include shots of his own family engaged in leisure time activities. As Merali describes it, the installation was

> …wholly derived from my polarised native/tourist experiences of visiting Goa, India. This shattered wholeness, a minefield of cultural/personalised references could only be physically encountered through a reconstruction based on how one survives through 'one's own biases', the sense of nationalism or racial identity played a pivotal role, emerging as it does in the articulation and inscription of culture's hybridity.[28]

London artist **Zarina Bhimji** was born in Mbarara, Uganda. Her interest in researching and interacting with environments and institutions has led Bhimji to work in, and make photo-based work about, a variety of places ranging from a pathology museum in a London hospital to the Orientalist environment of Leighton House, home of Fredrick Lord Leighton, artist and president of the Royal Academy. Her work, *It is Like a Brightness in the Heart*, addresses the vital importance of having free access to books. It was photographed at the British Library, where, like Karl Marx and many others, Mohandas K. Gandhi found inspiration in the ideas of others.

Navin Rawanchaikul, who was born of Indian parents in Thailand, currently resides in Fukuoka, Japan. He says that his works focus on the relationship between art and everyday life, and that he is especially interested in offering ordinary people an opportunity to join in as part of a collective art experience. Rawanchaikul has asked members of the main temple, a vital meeting place for Indians of all generations in Chiang Mai, to write messages about their experiences of life in Thailand and mail them to the exhibition, *Out of India*. Visitors to the exhibition will have an opportunity to reply. Other collaborations Rawanchaikul has organized include: an exchange between schoolchildren in Atlanta, Georgia, Kwangju, South Korea, and Chiang Mai, Thailand; a cooperative venture between artist Rirkrit Tiravanija and 20 *Tuk-Tuk* [29] drivers in Chiang Mai; and projects for a taxicab that has housed Navin Gallery Bangkok and featured changing exhibitions by invited artists since 1994.

Through their work, artists in this exhibition challenge notions of identity, ethnicity, and the nation and provide insight into current cultural conditions both inside and outside of what once was colonial India.

Endnotes

1. See Sadanand Menon, "Honouring the 'Mother' of Indian Photographers," *Economic Times New Delhi,* 12 September 1993, 12.

2. See Geeta Kapur, "Dismantling the Norm," *Contemporary Art in Asia: Traditions/Tensions* (New York: Asia Society Galleries, 1996), 60-61.

3. See Ranjit Hoskote, *Private Languages* (Mumbai: Pundole Art Gallery, 1997), 3-4.

4. From Sau-Ling C. Wong, "Denationalization Reconsidered: Asian American Cultural Criticism at a Theoretical Crossroads," *Amerasia Journal* 21, nos. 1, 2 (1995): 1-27.

5. Kapur, 60-61.

6. Nalini Malani as quoted by Kamala Kapoor, "Nalini Malani: Missives from the Streets," *ARTAsia Pacific* 2, no.1 (1995): 51.

7. Babari Masjid (1528) was a mosque built during the Mughal Dynasty said to have replaced a Hindu temple commemorating Rama's birthplace. In 1856, the British put a railing around the mosque and built a platform outside for Hindu worship and allowed Muslims to continue to pray inside. The government closed the site to both communities in 1947. Hindus placed Rama's image in the mosque in 1949, giving rise to a rumor that Lord Rama had appeared to claim his temple. Riots ensued, but the image was never removed, and Hindus and Muslims both sued to lay claim to the site.

    In 1984 the Vishva Hindu Parishad (VHP), a Hindu nationalist movement, demanded the site be reopened, which was granted by a 1986 court order, setting off communal violence all over north India. In September 1989, the VHP began organizing processions to bring "sacred bricks" to Ayodhya to build a temple in place of the mosque. Some 300 lives were lost, many in Bihar where the Muslim population of Bhagalpur was decimated. However, the VHP was allowed to lay its foundation stones — many of which came from the United States, Canada, the Caribbean, and South Africa — outside the mosque on so-called undisputed lands.

    In 1990, extreme violence erupted against the Hindu population in Kashmir; and riots were widespread when V.P. Singh's government increased the number of reserved places for the scheduled castes. Lal Kishan Advani, leader of the Bharatiya Janata party (BJP),which was allied with the Rahtriya Swayamsevak Sangh (RSS) and the VHP—both Hindu nationalist movements—started on a ritual procession from Somanatha in Gujarat to Ayodhya to construct the new temple to Rama on October 30. He was arrested in Bihar, but his followers marched on to the mosque, stopping only when police opened fire. V.P. Singh's government lost the BJP's support in parliament and fell on November 16.

    The VHP launched a video and audio cassette campaign about the October 30 events in Ayodhya claiming police killed thousands and suppressed the evidence. Ashes of Ayodhya martyrs were carried throughout the country in a ritual campaign. This brought victory to the BJP in the 1991 elections, and led to a BJP government in Uttar Pradesh. The VHP continued to demand the mosque be demolished to build the temple, and on

December 6, 1992, a VHP and BJP rally in Ayodhya resulted in the destruction of the Babari Masjid.

The Indian government imposed president's rule in Uttar Pradesh, and dismissed BJP governments in Madhya Pradesh, Himachal Pradesh, and Rajasthan. Prime minister, P.V. Narasimha Rao expressed the government's intention to rebuild the mosque, and banned the RSS and VHP and other Hindu organizations. The mosque's destruction provoked tremendous communal violence, especially in Bombay, Ahmedabad, Surat, and Calcutta. See Peter van der Veer, *Religious Nationalism: Hindus and Muslims in India* (Berkeley and Los Angeles: University of California Press, 1994), 2-7. In September 1997, an Indian court charged 49 Hindu politicians and religious leaders with rioting and criminal conspiracy in connection with the mosque's demolition. From Agence France-Presse, "49 Hindu leaders in Indian dock over Babri mosque razing," *Netcom WebNews*, 9 September 1997.

8. John F. Burns, "India's 5 Decades of Progress and Pain," *New York Times International*, 14 August 1997, A11.

9. See van der Veer, 8-9.

10. See Nigel Harris, *The New Untouchables: Immigration and the New World Worker* (London: Penguin Books, 1995), 16, 20.

11. Netaji Subhashchandra Bose was an Indian military leader who joined the Japanese against the British during World War II.

12. The participation of the police in the attacks on Muslims has also been documented in other areas, such as the east Delhi neighborhood of Seelampur. The events in India had, moreover, international repercussions. In Pakistan, Bangladesh, and Great Britain, Muslims rioted and set fire to Hindu temples in retaliation. See van der Veer, 2-7

13. Christianity was said to have been brought to India by St. Thomas the Apostle around A.D. 54. The ancient Syrian Orthodox Church in Kerala regards him as its founder, and he is said to be buried in St. Thome Cathedral in Madras. In the 16th and 17th centuries, Jesuit missionaries came to Goa with the Portuguese; and evangelical missionaries from London arrived in Calcutta, Bombay, and Madras after 1813 when the ban on missionary travel to and settlement in India was lifted. Fewer than one percent of the population converted, most of whom were outcastes or poor Muslims, called "rice Christians." Conversion meant expulsion from one's caste, and a man expelled from his caste was also automatically expelled from his family, unless they accompanied him in his social ostracism. A.L. Basham, *The Wonder That Was India* (New Delhi: Rupa & Co., 1994), 151.

14. Ayisha Abraham, from a paper presented at the conference *Art Object in a Postmodern World* at the Mohile Parikh Center for the Visual Arts, Mumbai, 1996.

15. Castes are groups of people united by customs and endogamy (marriage within the group) and by common and hereditary occupations. Within the four main castes in India, Brahmans (priestly), Kshatriyas (warrior), Vaishyas (mercantile), and Sudra (laboring), are approximately 3,000 other castes.

16. Shashi Tharoor, *India: From Midnight to the Millennium* (New York: Arcade, 1997), 106-107.

17. *Krisha Veni* means "the dark plaited one," and is a popular name among women in Andhra Pradesh. It also has the meaning of one who loves Lord Krishna.

18. Wong, 1-27.

19. See Geeta Kapur's "Elegy for an Unclaimed Beloved: Nasreen Mohamedi (1937-1990)" in Altaf, ed., *Nasreen in Retrospect* (Bombay: Ashraf Mohamedi Trust, 1995), 12-19.

20. Samena Rana as quoted in *Crossing Black Waters* (London: Panchayat, 1991), 64.

21. See Sonali Fernando, "Hair of the Dog? Perspectives on Artists of South Asian Heritage Descent in Britain," *Fuse Magazine* 18 (1994): 18.

22. From an artist's statement, 1996.

23. From an artist's statement, 1996.

24. See Dana Friis-Hansen in *Transculture: La Biennale de Venezia 1995* (Tokyo: The Japan Foundation, 1995), 132.

25. From an artist's statement, 1997.

26. Native Fijians are 46 percent of the population while Indians descended from field workers brought by the British make up nearly 50 percent. Indians are forbidden land ownership, but operate most sugar plantations. Linguistic and religious differences exist between the two groups. In May 1987, the Fijian-dominated National Alliance party lost to an Indian-backed coalition, prompting a military coup by Lieutenant Colonel Sitiveni Rabuka. The Supreme Court declared the coup illegal, and the governor-general who assumed power wanted to establish a caretaker government representing all. This led to another coup by Rabuka, who declared Fiji a republic and turned it over to a civilian government on December 5. In 1990, a constitution guaranteeing Fijians a permanent legislative majority was approved.

27. *Going Native* soundtrack was composed by Merali in collaboration with musician Oni Ruddha Das of Asian Dub Foundation (ADF).

28. From an artist's statement, 1995.

29. A *tuk-tuk* is a three-wheeled vehicle that is used as a taxi.

Ayisha Abraham
...looks the other way:
...looks the other way,
1993-94

Ayisha Abraham

Born in 1963, London, UK
Lives in Bangalore, India

Education

1995 MFA in Painting, Rutgers University,
New Brunswick, NJ
1993 MFA in Painting, Pratt Institute,
Brooklyn, NY
1992 Whitney Independent Study Program,
New York, NY
1990 Art Students League, New York, NY
1987 BFA, Faculty of Fine Arts, MS, University
of Baroda, India

Selected Solo Exhibitions

1995 *...looks the other way*, Franklin Furnace,
New York, NY
The Migration of Memory, The Brecht
Forum, New York, NY
1992 *Migrating Selves-Race-ing Histories*, Art in
General, New York, NY

Selected Group Exhibitions

1997 *Mappings: shared histories...a fragile self*,
Eicher Gallery, New Delhi, India (catalogue)
*Telling Tales: Five Contemporary Women
Artists*, Victoria Art Gallery, Bath, UK
*Telling Times: Five Contemporary Women
Artists*, British Council, New Delhi, India
1996 *Three Asian Artists*, Z Gallery, New York, NY
1994 *Art Studio*, Desh Pradesh, Toronto, Canada
1992 *Choice Histories*, Artists Space, New York, NY
Open Studio, Whitney Independent Study
Program, New York, NY

Mohini Chandra
Album Pacifica, 1997

Mohini Chandra

Born in 1964, Canvey Island near London, UK
Lives in London, UK

Education

1997 Ph.D. candidate, Photography/Humanity,
Royal College of Art, London, UK
1994 BFA in Photography, West Surrey College of
Art, Farnham, UK
1992 Diploma in Photography, University of
Westminster, London, UK
1985 BA in Sociology, University of Queensland,
Brisbane, Australia

Selected Solo Exhibitions

1997 Bluecoat Gallery, Liverpool, UK (catalogue)
1996 Old Post Office/Zone Gallery, Newcastle, UK

Selected Group Exhibitions

1997 *Dislocations*, International Triennale, Finland
(catalogue)
Standpoint Gallery, Hoxton Square,
London, UK
1996 Tom Blau Gallery, London, UK
Royal College of Art, London, UK
1995 1st Johannesburg Biennale, Johannesburg,
South Africa (catalogue)
Institute of Modern Art, Brisbane, Australia
Living the War, Brisbane City Council,
Australia (touring)
1994 *Occupying Territories*, Zone Gallery,
Newcastle, UK (catalogue)
de Composure, North London, London, UK
1993 The South Bank Photo Show, London, UK

Atul Dodiya

Born in 1959, Bombay, India
Lives in Ghat Kopar, Mumbai, India

Atul Dodiya
2nd October,
1993

Education
1982   BFA, Sir J.J. School of Art, Bombay, India

Selected Solo Exhibitions
1997   *Recent Works*, Gallery Chemould, Mumbai,
       India, and CIMA Gallery, Calcutta, India
       (catalogue)
1995   *Oil Paintings*, Gallery Chemould, Bombay,
       India (catalogue)
1989/91 Gallery Chemould, Bombay, India
1993   Gallery Apunto, Amsterdam, Holland

Selected Group Exhibitions
1993   *Trends and Images*, CIMA Gallery,
       Calcutta, India
       Reflections and Images, Vadhera Art Gallery,
       New Delhi and Bombay, India
1992   *Husain Ki Sarai*, Husain Museum, organized
       by Vadhera Art Gallery, New Delhi, India
       Exposition Collective-Cité Internationale des
       Arts, Paris, France
1991   *State of the Art*, Jehangir Art Gallery,
       Bombay, India
1990   *Gadhyaparva Exhibition*, Gallery Chemould,
       Bombay, India
1989/90 *The Richness of the Spirit: Selections of
       Contemporary Figurative Indian Art*, National
       Museum, Kuwait, and Egyptian Academy,
       Rome, Italy
       India — Contemporary Art, World Trade
       Center, Amsterdam, Holland
       Artist Alert, Safdar Hashmi Memorial Trust,
       New Delhi, India
1989   *Indian Eclectics*, sponsored by French
       Embassy and Sankriti Pratisthan, New
       Delhi, India

Vijay Kumar
India Portfolio, 1993

Vijay Kumar

Born in 1942, Lahore, India
Lives in Brooklyn, NY

Education
1967   Triveni Kala Sangam, New Delhi, India

Selected Solo Exhibitions
1997   L.T.G. Gallery, New Delhi, India
1995   Bose Pacia Modern Gallery, New York, NY
1993   Manhattan Graphics Center, New York, NY
1970   Hammond Gallery, Pennsylvania State
       University, State College, PA
1969   Kunstzaal Polder, Den Haag, The
       Netherlands
1967   Baladiya Hall, Basrah, Iraq
       The Society of Iraqi Artists Building,
       Baghdad, Iraq

Selected Goup Exhibitions
1997   *Swarajya*, Gallery at 678, New York, NY
       New Horizons, Bankside Gallery, London, UK
1996   *Hand matters*, Kingsborough Community
       College Art Gallery, Brooklyn, NY
       Paper Transformed, Connecticut Graphic Art
       Center, Norwalk, CT
       Mini Print '96, Gallery Espace, New Delhi,
       India (touring)
1995   *The Traditional and the Unacknowledged*,
       Condeso/Lawler Gallery, New York, NY
       Postcards for Gandhi, Sahmat, New Delhi,
       India (touring)
1994   *Contemporary Indian Artists*, Permanent
       Mission of India, New York, NY
1993   *We Count! The State of Asian Pacific America*,
       Tweed Gallery, New York, NY

Nalini Malani
Control, 1993

Nalini Malani

Born in 1946, Karachi, India
Lives in Mumbai, India

Education
1969   Diploma in Fine Arts, Sir J.J. School of Art, Bombay, India
1964   Bhulabhai Memorial Institute, Bombay, India

Selected Solo Exhibitions
1996   "Free Trade," *Container '96 - Art Across Oceans*, Copenhagen, Denmark (catalogue)
       Medea Installation, Max Mueller Bhavan, Mumbai, India
1995   *Bloodlines*, Gallery Chemould, Bombay, India (catalogue)
1992   *Site-Specific*, Gallery Chemould, Bombay, India
1991   *Hieroglyphs*, Gallery Chemould/Jehangir Art Gallery, Bombay, India (touring)
       City of Desires, Gallery Chemould, Bombay, India
1990   *Under the Skin*, Gallery 7, Bombay, India
1983   Contemporary Art Gallery, Ahmedabad, India
1982/84/86 Pundole Art Gallery, Bombay, India
1980   Art Heritage, New Delhi, India (catalogue)

Selected Group Exhibitions
1997   *Mappings: shared histories...a fragile self*, Eicher Gallery, New Delhi, India (catalogue)
1996   *Traditions/Tensions: Contemporary Art in Asia*, Asia Society/Grey Art Gallery, New York, NY (catalogue/touring)
       The 2nd Asia Pacific Triennial of Contemporary Art, Queensland Art Gallery, Brisbane, Australia (catalogue)
1995   *Postcards for Gandhi*, Sahmat Exhibition, New Delhi, India (touring)
       Inside-Out: Contemporary Women Artists of India, Middlesbrough Art Gallery, Middlesbrough, UK
       Africus, 1st Johannesburg Biennale, Johannesburg, South Africa (catalogue)
1994   *Parallel Perceptions*, Sakshi Gallery, Bombay, India
1993   *A Critical Difference: Contemporary Art from India*, Chapter Arts Centre, Cardiff, Wales, UK (catalogue/touring)
1991   *Artists Against Communalism*, Safdar Hashmi Memorial Trust, New Delhi, India (catalogue/touring)

1989   *Artist Alert*, Lalit Kala Galleries, New Delhi, India
1988   *Through the Looking Glass*, Bharat Bhavan, Bhopal, India (touring)
1987   *2nd Bienal de la Habana*, National Museum, Havana, and Smith Galleries, London, UK
1982   *Contemporary Indian Art*, Festival of India 1982, Royal Academy of Arts, London, UK
       Myth and Reality, Museum of Modern Art, Oxford, UK
1980   *Place for People*, Jehangir Art Gallery, Bombay, and Rabindra Bhavan, New Delhi, India

Shaheen Merali
Slide Projection from
Going Native, 1992

Shaheen Merali

Born in 1959, Dar es Salaam, Tanzania
Lives in London, UK

Education
1986 Adult Education Willesden College,
      London, UK
1982 B.A. in Sculpture, Gwent College of Further
      Education, South Wales, UK
1979 Foundation Course, Barnet College,
      London, UK

Selected Solo Exhibitions
1995 *Paradigms Lost*, Travelling Gallery, Scotland
      (touring)
1994 *Torchlights*, Brick Lane Police Station, East
      London, UK
1993 *Channels, Echoes and Empty Chairs*, Angel
      Row Gallery, Nottingham and South
      London Gallery, London, UK
1989 *The Fire and the Garden*, Tom Allen Centre,
      London, UK

Selected Group Exhibitions
1997 *Translocation*, The Photographers' Gallery,
      London, UK
      *Transforming the Crown: African, Asian, and
      Caribbean Artists in Britain 1966-1996*, The
      Caribbean Cultural Center/Bronx Museum
      of the Arts, Bronx, NY (catalogue/touring)
      Alien/Nation, Sixpack Films, Vienna, Austria
      Musée Imaginaire, The Museum of
      Installation, London, UK
1996 *Under Different Skies*, Oksenhallen,
      Copenhagen, Denmark
1995 *Heaven*, Prema Arts Centre, Gloucester, UK
1994 *Melting Pots*, The Tate, St. Ives, Cornwall, UK
1993 *Beyond Destinations*, Ikon Gallery,
      Birmingham, UK (touring)
      25th Anniversary of *Time Out* magazine,
      Billboard Commission in Ealing, London, UK
      Forensic Fictions, ICA, London, UK
1992 *Trophies of Empire*, Bluecoat, Liverpool, and
      Arnolfini, Bristol, UK
1991 *Fire, Theft and Acts of Gods*, Angel Row
      Gallery, Nottingham, UK (touring)
      Crossing Black Waters, City Gallery, Leicester,
      UK (catalogoue/touring)
1990 *Distinguishing Marks,* Bloomsbury Gallery,
      University of London, UK
1989 *Fabled Territories*, Leeds City Art Gallery,
      Leeds, UK (touring)
      3rd Bienal de la Habana, Havana, Cuba

Nasreen Mohamedi
Untitled, undated

Nasreen Mohamedi

Born in 1937, Karachi, India
Died 1990

Education
1957 Diploma in Design, St. Martin's School of
Art, London, UK

Selected Solo Exhibitions
1991 Jehangir Art Gallery, Bombay, India
1989 Jehangir Art Gallery, Bombay, India
1982 Prithvi Art Gallery, Bombay, India
1981 Shridharani Art Gallery, New Delhi, India
1977 Jehangir Art Gallery, Bombay, India
1976 Black Partridge, New Delhi, India
1974 Jehangir Art Gallery, Bombay, India
1969 British Council, Bahrain
1968 The Taj Art Gallery, Bombay, India
1963 Gallery Chemould, Bombay, India
1961 Gallery 59, Bombay, India

Selected Group Exhibitions
1985 *Artistes Indiens en France*, Paris, France
1982 *Contemporary Indian Art*, Festival of India,
London, UK
1977 *Pictorial Space*, The Lalit Kala Akademi,
New Delhi, India
1975 3rd Triennale, New Delhi, India
1970 Lalit Kala Akademi National Exhibition,
New Delhi, India
Art Today - II, New Delhi, India

Navin Rawanchaikul

Born in 1971, Chiang Mai, Thailand
Lives in Chiang Mai, Thailand, and Fukuoka, Japan

Navin Rawanchaikul
*from Chiang Mai on
September 28, 1997*

Education
1994 BFA, Chiang Mai University, Chiang Mai,
Thailand

Selected Solo Exhibitions
1997 *Navin and His Gang (Visit) Vancouver*,
Contemporary Art Gallery, Vancouver,
Canada
1995 *The Zero Space which is Not Empty*, Art
Forum Gallery, Bangkok, Thailand
SUBSTANCEABOUTNONSUBSTANCE,
Goethe Institute, Bangkok, Thailand
1994 *There is No Voice*, The AUA Language
Center Library, Bangkok, Thailand
(catalogue)

Selected Group Exhibitions
1997 *Cities on the Move*, Wiener Secession,
Vienna, Austria (catalogue)
Hibridity, 2nd Kwangju Biennale, Kwangju,
South Korea (catalogue)
*Art in Southeast Asia 1997: Glimpses into the
Future*, Museum of Contemporary Art,
Tokyo, and Hiroshima City Museum of
Contemporary Art, Hiroshima, Japan
1996 *Asia Modern Collection*, Fukuoka Art
Museum, Fukuoka, Japan
*The 2nd Asia-Pacific Triennial of
Contemporary Art*, Queensland Art Gallery,
Brisbane, Australia
Traditions/Tensions: Contemporary Art in Asia,
Asia Society/Queens Museum of Art, NY
(catalogue/touring)
1995 *Thai/Tensions*, Chulalongkorn Art Gallery,
Bangkok, Thailand (catalogue)
Art and Environment 3, National Gallery,
Bangkok, Thailand
1994 *4th Asian Art Show: Realism as an Attitude*,
Fukuoka Art Museum, Fukuoka, Japan
(catalogue/touring)
1993 *Art and Environment II*, National Gallery,
Bangkok, Thailand
Social Contract: New Art from Chiang Mai,
Visual Dhamma Gallery, Bangkok, Thailand

Satish Sharma
From *Deconstructing the
Politician,* 1990-96

Satish Sharma

Born in 1951, Nilgiri Hills, Tamil Nadu, India
Lives in New Delhi, India

Selected Solo Exhibitions
1997 Eicher Gallery, New Delhi, India
1990 Center for Photography as a Fine Art,
          NCPA, Bombay, India
1987 Cholamandal Artists Village Gallery,
          Cholamandal, India
          Sakshi Gallery, Madras, India
1986 Art Heritage, New Delhi, India (catalogue)

Selected Group Exhibitions
1997 *Mappings: shared histories...a fragile self*, Eicher
          Gallery, New Delhi, India (catalogue)
1995 *Project Punjab*, National Gallery of Modern
          Art, New Delhi, India
1991 *Artists Against Communalism*, Safdar
          Hashmi Memorial Trust, New Delhi, India
          (catalogue/touring)
1989 *Artist Alert*, Rabindra Bhavan, New Delhi,
          India (catalogue)
          *Working News Cameramens' Association
          Members Exhibition*, AIFACS Gallery,
          New Delhi, India
1988 *Pratibimba*, Pushkin Museum, Moscow,
          USSR (Festival of India) (catalogue)
1987 *Les Photographes Indiens Contemporains*,
          Musée de l'Elysée, Lausanne, Switzerland
1985 *Photographing India*, International Center of
          Photography, New York, NY

Dayanita Singh
Samara Chopra and Her
Friend Pooja Dress Alike for
a Photograph Lesson and
Deen Dayal, the Caretaker,
is Amazed at How Quickly
They Have Grown, 1997

Dayanita Singh

Born in 1961, New Delhi, India
Lives in New Delhi, India

Education
1986 Diploma in Visual Communications,
National Institute of Design, Ahmedabad,
India
1988 Photojournalism and Documentary,
International Center for Photography,
New York, NY

Selected Solo Exhibitions
1997 *Dayanita Singh: Images from the 90's*, Scalo,
Zurich, Switzerland

Selected Group Exhibitions
1997/98 *India: A Celebration of Independence*,
Philadelphia Museum of Art, Philadelphia,
PA (catalogue/touring)
1997 *India: A Contemporary View*, Asian Arts
Museum, San Francisco, CA
50 Years and the Indian Woman, Delhi,
India (touring)
Canon Top Ten Photographers, Delhi,
India (touring)
Patient Planet: a World History through Photos
from DU Magazine, 1941-1995 (touring)

Homai Vyarawalla
Mahatma Gandhi was assassinated on the 30th January, 1948. Picture shows, among others, Mr. Nehru and Lord Mountbatten getting the body ready on the army cortege for the funeral procession in Delhi the next day.

Homai Vyarawalla

Born in 1913, Navsari-Gujarat, India
Lives in Vadodara (Gujarat), India

Education

Economics, St. Xavier's College,
Bombay, India
Painting, Sir J.J. School of Art,
Bombay, India

Selected Solo Exhibitions

1994　Piramal Gallery, National Center for the
Performing Arts, Bombay, India
1993　Max Mueller Bhavan, New Delhi, India
(catalogue)

Zarina
Homes I Made/A Life in
Nine Lines: Paris, 1997

Zarina

Born in 1937, Aliganh, India
Lives in New York, NY

Education

1958 BS, Aliganh Muslim University, Aliganh,
      India

Selected Solo Exhibitions

1994 *Homes I Made*, Faculty Gallery, University of
      California at Santa Cruz, CA
1993 Chawkandi Gallery, Karachi, Pakistan
1992 *House with Four Walls*, Bronx Museum of the
      Arts, Bronx, NY
1990 Roberta English Gallery, San Francisco, CA
1986 Art Heritage, New Delhi, India
1985 Women Artist Series, Rutgers University,
      New Brunswick, NJ
1983 Satori Gallery, San Francisco, CA
1981 Herbert F. Johnson Museum of Art,
      Ithaca, NY
1977 Gallery Alana, Oslo, Norway

Selected Group Exhibitions

1997 *India and Pakistan Contemporary Prints*,
      Victoria and Albert Museum, London, UK
      Gift from India, Sahmat Lalit Kala
      Akedemi, New Delhi, India
1996 *25 Years of Feminism/25 Years of Women's
      Art*, Mason Gross School of Art Gallery,
      Rutgers University, New Brunswick, NJ
      Mini Print, Gallery Espace, New Delhi,
      India
1995 *Arts and Letters*, June Kelly Gallery, New
      York, NY
      International Biennial of Prints, Bhopal,
      India
1994 *International Print Triennial and
      Intergrafica*, Cracow, Poland
      *Asia/America: Identities in Contemporary
      Asian American Art*, The Asia Society, New
      York, NY
1992 *From Bonnard to Baselitz: From Print
      Collection*, Bibliothèque Nationale, Paris,
      France
1988 *The Language of Form: The Form of
      Language*, Rosa Esman Gallery,
      New York, NY
1985 *Ripe Fruit*, P.S. 1, Long Island City, NY

Rina Banjerjee
Home within a Harem (detail),
1997

Rina Banerjee

Born in 1963, Calcutta, India
Lives in State College, PA, and Brooklyn, NY

Education
1995   MFA in Painting and Printmaking, Yale
       University, New Haven, CT
1993   BS in Polymer Engineering, Case Western
       Reserve University, Cleveland, OH

Selected Exhibitions
1997   *Fermented*, Parsons School of Art Gallery,
       New York, NY
       Color Schemes, Axis Gallery, Philadelphia, PA
1996   *Artists in the Marketplace*, Bronx Museum of
       the Arts, Bronx, NY (catalogue)
       In Full Bloom, ONS Gallery, New York,
       NY (catalogue)
1995   *Intuitive Mixed Media*, Middle Tennessee
       State University Gallery, Murfreesboro, TN
       New Work '95, ArtSpace Gallery,
       New Haven, CT
       Leonardo's Clothespin, Eli Whitney Museum,
       New Haven, CT
1994   *Toma Mi Carozon*, La Pena Gallery, Austin, TX
       Aids, Yale Art Gallery, New Haven, CT
1993   *Answer to the Rhythm of Your Drum*, Pacific
       Arts Center, Seattle, WA
       One Voice, Insights Gallery, Seattle, WA

Pablo Bartholomew
*Indians in America: South
Asian Muslims Pray during
Id at Corona Park, Flushing
Meadows, Queens, New York,*
1988

Pablo Bartholomew

Born in 1955, Tavoy, Burma
Lives in New Delhi, India

Education
Self-taught

Selected Solo Exhibitions
1994 *The Indian Emigré*, Centre of Photographic
      Arts (CPA), Bombay, India
1985 Museum of Modern Art, Oxford, UK
      International Center of Photography,
      New York, NY
1982 The Photographers' Gallery, London, UK
1980 Jehangir Art Gallery, Bombay, India

Selected Group Exhibitions
1997 *A Contemporary View*, Asian Arts Museum,
      San Francisco, CA
1991 *Ten Thousand Eyes*, International Center for
      Photography, New York, NY
      (catalogue/touring)
1980 Art Heritage Gallery, New Delhi, India

Zarina Bhimji
*It is Like a Brightness in the
Heart,* 1997

Zarina Bhimji

Born in 1963, Mbarara, Uganda
Lives in London, UK

Education
1989 MFA in Mixed Media, Slade School of
Fine Art, University College London,
London, UK
1986 BA in Fine Art, Goldsmiths' College School
of Art and Design, London, UK
1983 Art Foundation, Leicester Polytechnic,
Leicester, UK

Selected Solo Exhibitions
1995 Kettles Yard, University of Cambridge,
Cambridge, UK (catalogue)
1992 *I will always be here*, Ikon Gallery,
Birmingham, UK (catalogue)
1989 Tom Allen Community Art Centre,
London, UK
Slade School of Fine Art, University College
London, London, UK
1986 Goldsmiths' College School of Art and
Design, London, UK

Selected Group Exhibitions
1997 *no place (like home)*, Walker Arts Center,
Minneapolis, MN (catalogue)
Life's Little Necessities, 2nd Johannesburg
Biennale, Johannesburg, South Africa
(catalogue)
British Contemporary Photography, NGBK
Photography Group, Berlin, Germany
(catalogue/touring)

1996 *In/sight: African Photographers, 1940 to the
Present*, Solomon R. Guggenheim Museum,
New York, NY (catalogue)
1995 *The Impossible Science of Being*, The
Photographers' Gallery, London, UK
(catalogue)
1991 *Shocks to the System,* South Bank Centre,
London, UK (touring)
1990 *Fabled Territories*, Leeds City Art Gallery,
Leeds, UK (touring)
Selections 5, Photokina, '90, Cologne,
Germany (touring)
*Black Markets: Images of black people in
advertising*, Cornerhouse, Manchester, UK
(touring)
Intimate Distance, The Photographers'
Gallery, London, UK (catalogue/touring)
1989 *Towards a Bigger Picture*, Victoria and Albert
Museum, London, UK (touring)
1988 *The Essential BLACK ART*, Chisenhale
Gallery, London, UK (touring)
1987 *The Image Employed: The Use of Narrative in
Black Art*, Cornerhouse, Manchester, UK
Dislocation, Kettles Yard, University of
Cambridge, Cambridge, UK

Chila Kumari Burman
*Fly Girl Watching the World,
Auto-Portrait,* 1993

Chila Kumari Burman

Born in 1957, Liverpool, UK
Lives in London, UK

Education

1982 MFA in Printmaking, Slade School of
Fine Art, University College London,
London, UK
1980 BA in Fine Art and Graphic Art, Leeds
Metropolitan University, Leeds, UK
1976 Foundation Course, Southport College of
Art and Design, Southport, UK

Selected Solo Exhibitions

1997 *Ice Cream and Magic*, Peoples Museum,
Manchester, UK
1996 *Between the Visible and the Invisible*, Lahore
College of Art, Pakistan
Pop, Mass n' Subculture, Banff Centre for the
Arts, Banff, Canada
1995 Watermans Arts Centre, London, UK
28 Positions in 34 Years, Camerawork,
London, UK (touring)
1993 *Body Weapons*, Seven Vintappres GR3,
Stockholm, Sweden

Selected Group Exhibitions

1997 *Transforming the Crown: African, Asian, and
Caribbean Artists in Britain 1966-1996*, The
Caribbean Cultural Center/Studio Museum
in Harlem, New York, NY (catalogue/touring)
1996 *Face Value*, University of Essex Gallery,
Essex, UK
1995 *Right to Hope*, Johannesburg Art Gallery,
Johannesburg, South Africa
Photo-Genetic: Reviewing the Lens of History,
Street Level Gallery, Glasgow, Scotland
1994 *With Your Own Face on It*, Plymouth Arts
Centre, UK (touring)
5th Bienal de la Habana, Havana, Cuba
My Grandmother, My Mother, Myself,
Southampton City Art Gallery,
Southampton, UK (touring)
1993 *Transition of Riches*, Birmingham City
Museum and Art Gallery, Birmingham, UK
1992 *Fine Material for the Dream*, Harris Museum
and Art Gallery, Preston, UK
1991 *The Circular Dance*, Arnolfini, Bristol, UK
1990 *Fabled Territories*, Leeds City Art Gallery,
Leeds, UK (touring)

Poulomi Desai
*Shakti Queens: Vijiya Devi
and Meena* (detail), 1997

Poulomi Desai

Born in London, UK
Lives in London, UK

Selected Solo Exhibitions

1997 *from the coffee table to the kit(s)chen* (cd rom
exhibition), Autograph, London, UK

1996 *from the coffee table to the kit(s)chen*,
Autograph, London, UK, and The Oxford
Gallery, Calcutta, India, (catalogue)

Selected Group Exhibitions

1997 Online exhibition
@http://www.lmu.ac.uk/ces/axis
Translocations, The Photographers' Gallery
and Displaced Data, London, UK
(catalogue)

1987 *Images: Photographic Expressions of the
Commonwealth*, Commonwealth Institute,
London, UK (catalogue/touring)

1992 *Onno Choke Dheka*,
Autograph/Drik/Camerawork, London, UK,
and Dhaka, Bangladesh

1990 *Fabled Territories*. Leeds City Art Gallery,
Leeds, UK (catalogue)

1985 *Garam Masala*, Southall Asian and
Afro-Caribbean Arts Collective, London,
UK (touring)

1984 *Gurjar*, Hackney Asian Association,
London, UK

Allan deSouza
Lady Asia, 1997

Allan deSouza

Born in 1958, Nairobi, Kenya
Lives in Los Angeles, CA

Education

1997 MFA in Photography, UCLA, Los Angeles, CA
1994 Critical Studies, Whitney Independent Studies Program, New York, NY
1983 BA in Fine Art, Bath Academy of Art, Bath, UK
1977 Foundation Art, Goldsmiths' College School of Art and Design, London, UK

Selected Solo Exhibitions

1997 *Threshold*, Highways, Santa Monica, CA
1989 Kafe Klatsch, Wiesbaden, Germany

Selected Group Exhibitions

1997 *Translocations*, The Photographers' Gallery, London; City University of New York, NY
Transforming the Crown: African, Asian, and Caribbean Artists in Britain 1966-1996, The Caribbean Cultural Center/Studio Museum in Harlem, New York, NY (catalogue/touring)
Kimchee Extravaganza, Korean American Museum, Los Angeles, CA
AlterNatives, Lightworks Gallery, Syracuse, NY (catalogue)

1995 *Fire without Gold*, MTA/Arts for Transit and Organization of Independent Artists, New York, NY
1994 *Picturing Asia America*, Houston Center for Photography, Houston, TX
alter idem/performing personae, Camerawork, London, UK;
Beyond the Borders, Bronx Museum of the Arts, Bronx, NY (catalogue)
1993 *Artists in the Marketplace*, Bronx Museum of the Arts, Bronx, NY (catalogue)
1992 *Crossing Black Waters,* City Gallery, Leicester, UK (catalogue/touring)
1991 *Interrogating Identity*, Grey Art Gallery, New York, NY (catalogue/touring)
1990 *Distinguishing Marks*, Institute of Education, London, UK (catalogue)
1989 *Fabled Territories*, Leeds City Art Gallery, Leeds, UK (catalogue/touring)
3rd Bienal de la Habana, Havana, Cuba (catalogue)

Sunil Gupta
From *TRESPASS 3,* 1995

Sunil Gupta

Born in 1953, New Delhi, India
Lives in London, UK

Education

1983 MA in Photography, Royal College of Art,
London, UK
1981 Photography, West Surrey College of Art
and Design, Farnham, UK
1976 The New School for Social Research,
New York, NY
1976 Concordia University, Montreal, Canada
1972 Dawson College, Montreal, Canada

Selected Solo Exhibitions

1995-97 *TRESPASS 3*, Focal Point Gallery,
Southend, UK (touring)
1995 *TRESPASS 1*, Contemporary Art Gallery,
Vancouver, Canada (catalogue)
1991 Film in the Cities, St. Paul, MN
Theatre Workshop, Edinburgh, UK
(Festival)
1988 *Social Security*, The Showroom, London, UK

Selected Group Exhibitions

1997 *Transforming the Crown: African, Asian, and
Caribbean Artists in Britain 1966-1996*, The
Caribbean Cultural Center/Bronx Museum
of the Arts (catalogue/touring)
1994 *5th Bienal de la Habana*, National Museum,
Havana, Cuba, and Ludwig Forum, Aachen,
Germany
1993 *They Call it Love*, NGBK, Berlin, Germany
1992-93 *Trophies of Empire*, Bluecoat, Liverpool,
and Arnolfini, Bristol, UK
1992 *Fine Material for a Dream*, Harris Museum,
Preston, UK (touring)
Queer Landscape, Evergreen State College,
Olympia, WA
1991 *Shocks to the System*, South Bank Centre,
London, UK (touring)
1990 *Post Morality*, Kettles Yard, Cambridge, UK
Autoportraits, Camerawork, London, UK
Ecstatic Antibodies, Impression Gallery of
Photography, York, UK (touring)
1989 *Fabled Territories*, Leeds City Art Gallery,
Leeds, UK (touring)
1987 *The Body Politic*, The Photographers'
Gallery, London, UK (touring)

Mariam Ishaque

Born in 1969, Karachi, Pakistan
Lives in New York, NY

Education
1996 Studio Program, Whitney Independent
Study Program, New York, NY
1993 MFA, Yale University School of Art,
New Haven, CT
1991 BA, Brandeis University, Waltham, MA
1990 Yale/Norfolk Program in Painting,
Norfolk, CT

Selected Group Exhibitions
1996 *The Salon Show*, Room Gallery,
New York, NY
Open Studio, Whitney Independent Study
Program, New York, NY
Osaka Triennale of Painting, Osaka
Foundation for Culture, Osaka, Japan
(catalogue)
1995 *Four Artists at the Harvard Business School*,
Soldiers Field Park, Boston, MA
1994 *New Art 94*, Kingston Gallery, Boston , MA
1993 *Thesis Show*, Yale University Art Gallery,
New Haven, CT

Permindar Kaur
Falling (detail), 1995

Permindar Kaur

Born in 1965, Nottingham, UK
Lives in London, UK

Education

1992   MFA, Glasgow School of Art, Glasgow, Scotland
1989   BFA, Sheffield City Polytechnic, Sheffield, UK

Selected Solo Exhibitions

1997   *Fetish*, Art Gallery of Windsor, Windsor, Ontario, Canada
       Secrets Must Circulate, Galeria Carles Poy, Barcelona, Spain
1996   *Cold Comfort*, Bluecoat Gallery, Liverpool, UK
       Cold Comfort I, Ikon Gallery, Birmingham, UK (catalogue)
       Cold Comfort II, Mead Gallery, Warwick Arts Centre, University of Warwick, Coventry, UK
       Intimate Realities, Expais d'art Contemporani, Barcelona, Spain
       Backspace, Galeria Alejandro Sales, Barcelona, Spain
1995   *Small Spaces*, Galleri Isidor, Malmo, Sweden
1994   *Hidden Witnesses*, Galleri Amidol, Gothenburg, Sweden
1993   *Red Earth*, Harris Museum and Art Gallery, Preston, UK
       Regions & Growth, British Council, Barcelona, Spain

Selected Group Exhibitions

1997   *Arco '97*, Galeria Carles Poy, Madrid, Spain
       Flexible Co-existence, Mito Annual '97, Art Tower Mito, Mito, Japan (catalogue)
       Krishna, The Divine Lover, Whitechapel Art Gallery, London, UK (touring)
       Strangely Familiar, Ikon Gallery, Birmingham, UK (touring)
       Contemporary British Art, Museum of Contemporary Art, Sydney, Australia (touring)
1996   *Falling*, Museo Salvador Vilaseca, Reus, Spain (catalogue)
1995   *My Bloody Valentine*, Real Art Foundation, Barcelona, Spain
       Por al buit/miedo al vacio, Galeria Carles Poy, Barcelona, Spain
       Veins, Galeria dels Angels, Barcelona, Spain
1994   *La Cambra Daurada*, La Capella de l'Antic Hospital de la Santa Creu, Barcelona, Spain
       Project for Europe, Ferry Kronberg, Copenhagen, Denmark
1993   *Asian Arts Festival*, Worcester City Art Gallery, Worcester, UK
1992   *BBC Billboard Art Project*, Cathedral St., Glasgow, Scotland
       BT New Contemporaries, Newlyn Orion Gallery, Penzance, UK (touring)

Shani Mootoo

Born in 1957, Dublin, Ireland; raised in Trinidad
Lives in Vancouver, Canada

Shani Mootoo
A Landscape of One's Own,
1995

Education
1980 BFA, University of Western Ontario,
London, Canada
1983 Emily Carr College of Art and Design,
Vancouver, Canada

Selected Solo Exhibitions
1995 *Video Viewpoint:Transing the Green*, Museum
of Modern Art, New York, NY
1994 *Photocopies and Videotapes*, The
Contemporary Art Gallery, Vancouver,
Canada (catalogue)

Selected Group Exhibitions
1997 *Topographies: Aspects of Recent British
Columbian Art*, Vancouver Art Gallery,
Vancouver, Canada (catalogue)
1996 *Urban Fictions*, Presentation House,
Vancouver, Canada (catalogue)
1995 *Transculture*, Palazzo Giustinian Lolin
(Fondazione Levi), Venice Biennale, Venice,
Italy (catalogue)
1994 *For Our Own Pleasure*, YYZ Art Gallery,
Toronto, Canada
1993 *Artropolis*, Woodwards, Vancouver, Canada
(catalogue)
Racey, Sexy, Chinese Cultural Center,
Vancouver, Canada (catalogue)
1992 *Memory and Desire: The Voices of 11 Women
of Culture*, Vancouver Art Gallery,
Vancouver, Canada

Samena Rana
From *Flow of Water,* 1990

Samena Rana

Born in 1955, Lahore, Pakistan
Died 1992, London, UK

Education

1992 BA in Photography and Filmmaking,
Polytechnic of Central London, London, UK

Selected Group Exhibitions

1995 London Regional Art and Historical
Museums, London, Canada
1992 *Crossing Black Waters*, City Gallery,
Leicester, UK (catalogue/touring)
1991 *Vision II*, Diorama, London, UK
The Bottom Drawer, Small Mansions,
London, UK
1990 *Fragmented Images of Self*, Peckham Leisure
Centre, London, UK
A Woman in My Life, Small Mansions,
London, UK

Ravinder G. Reddy

Born in 1956, Suryapet, Andhra Pradesh, India
Lives in Visakhapatnam, Andhra Pradesh, India

Ravinder G. Reddy
Family, 1997

Education

1984 Short Course Certificate in Ceramics, Royal
College of Art, London, UK
1983 Diploma in Art and Design, Goldsmiths'
College School of Art and Design,
London, UK
1980 BFA in Sculpture, Maharaha Sayajirao
University, Baroda, India

Selected Solo Exhibitions

1996 *Sculptures*, Art Today, New Delhi, India
(catalogue)
1991 *Painted Sculptures and Reliefs*, 1989-91, Sakshi
Gallery, Bangalore and Madras, India
(catalogue)
1990 Center for Contemporary Art, New Delhi,
India (catalogue)
1989 Max Mueller Bhavan, Hyderabad, India
(catalogue)
1982 Contemporary Art Gallery, Ahmedabad,
India

Selected Group Exhibitions

1997 *Tryst with Destiny-Art in Modern India 1947-
1997*, CIMA Calcutta at the Singapore Art
Museum, Singapore, Malaysia (catalogue)
*Directions: Emerging Trends of Contemporary
Indian Art*, Appa Rao Galleries, Madras at
the Air Gallery, London, UK (catalogue)
Private Languages, Pundole Art Gallery,
Mumbai, India (catalogue)
1996 *Traditions/Tensions: Contemporary Art in Asia*,
The Asia Society, New York, NY
(catalogue/touring)
1995 *Sculpture '95*, Gallery Espace at Lalit Kala
Galleries, New Delhi, India (catalogue)
1993 *India Songs: Multiple Streams in Contemporary
Indian Art*, Art Gallery of New South Wales,
Sydney, Australia (catalogue)
*A Critical Difference: Contemporary Art from
India*, Chapter Arts Centre, Cardiff Wales,
UK (catalogue/touring)
1992 *Heads*, Sakshi Gallery, Bombay, India
(catalogue)
1990 *3rd Biennale*, Bharat Bhavan, Bhopal, India
(catalogue)
1989 *Artist Alert*, Lalit Kala Galleries, New Delhi,
India (catalogue)

N. N. Rimzon
*Faraway from One Hundred
and Eight Feet,* 1995

N. N. Rimzon

Born in 1957, Kakkoor, Kerala, India
Lives in Trivandrum, India

Education
1989   MFA, Royal College of Arts, London, UK
1987   Studies in Sculpture, Maharaja Sayajirao
       University, Baroda, India
1982   BFA in Sculpture, College of Fine Arts,
       Trivandrum, India

Selected Solo Exhibitions
1994   Galerie Schoo, Foundation for Indian
       Artists, Amsterdam, The Netherlands
1993   *Sculpture and Drawings*, Art Heritage, New
       Delhi, India (catalogue)
1991   *Recent Sculpture and Drawings*, Art Heritage,
       New Delhi, India (catalogue)

Selected Group Exhibitions
1996-97   *Fire and Life*, Sakshi Gallery, Bangalore,
          India, and The Art Gallery of New South
          Wales, Sydney, Australia (catalogue/touring)
1996   *2nd Asia-Pacific Triennial of Contemporary
          Art*, Queensland Art Gallery, Brisbane,
          Australia
          *The New South: Contemporary Painting and
          Sculpture from South India*, Arnolfini Gallery,
          Bristol, UK (touring)
          *Traditions/Tensions: Contemporary Art in
          Asia*, The Asia Society, New York, NY
          (catalogue/touring)
1995   *Art and Nature*, Buddha Jayanti Park, New
          Delhi, India
          The Other Self, National Gallery of Modern
          Art, New Delhi/Stedelijk Museum,
          Amsterdam, The Netherlands (catalogue)
          Recent Trends in Contemporary Indian Art,
          Vadhera Gallery, New Delhi, India
          (catalogue)
1994   *Deutsche Bank Collection*, Bombay, India
          (catalogue)
          *One Hundred Years: from the National Gallery
          of Modern Art*, New Delhi, India (catalogue)

1993   *A Critical Difference: Contemporary Art from
       India*, Chapter Arts Centre, Cardiff, Wales,
       UK (catalogue/touring)
       Inbetween, 14th Venice Biennale, Venice,
       Italy (catalogue)
       *India Songs: Multiple Streams in Contemporary
       Indian Art*, Art Gallery of New South Wales,
       Sydney, Australia (catalogue/touring)
       *Prospect '93: An International Exhibition of
       Contemporary Art*, Frankfurt Kunstverinnad
       Schirn Kunsthalle, Frankfurt, Germany
       (catalogue)
       Trends and Images, Centre of International
       Modern Art, Calcutta, India (catalogue)
1991   *4th Bienal de la Habana*, Havana, Cuba
       (catalogue)
1988   *The Sculpted Image*, Festival of India, Nehru
       Centre, Bombay, India (catalogue)
1987   *Six Contemporary Artists from India*, Centre
       d'Art Contemporain, Geneva, Switzerland
       (catalogue)
1986   *6th Triennale India*, Lalit Kala Akademi,
       New Delhi, India (catalogue)
1985   *Seven Young Sculptors*, Rabindra Bhavan,
       New Delhi, India (catalogue)

Shahzia Sikander

Born in 1969, Lahore, Pakistan
Lives in Houston, TX

Shahzia Sikander
*Uprooted Order Series 3,
no. 1,* 1997

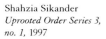

Education
1995 MFA, Rhode Island School of Design,
Providence, RI
1992 BFA, National College of Arts, Lahore,
Pakistan

Selected Solo Exhibitions
1997 Deitch Projects, New York, NY
Yerba Buena Gardens Center for the Arts,
San Francisco, CA
Beyond Surfaces, Hosfelt Gallery,
San Francisco, CA
1996 *Knock, Knock, Who's There Mithilia, Mithilia
Who?* Project Row Houses, Houston, TX
1995 *Fourth Space*, Gallery S.A.R.D., New York,
NY
1993 *Ordered Space*, Sol Koffler Gallery,
Washington, D. C.
Miniatures, Pakistan Embassy, Washington,
D. C.

Selected Group Exhibitions
1997 *Transversions*, 2nd Johannesburg Biennale,
Johannesburg, South Africa
Project Painting, Lehman Maupin Gallery,
New York, NY
Biennial Exhibition, The Whitney Museum
of American Art, New York, NY
Selections Spring '97, The Drawing Center,
New York, NY
Core 1997 Exhibition, Glassell School of Art,
Museum of Fine Arts, Houston, TX
Eastern Edge, Laing Gallery, Newcastle, UK
1996 *Core 1996 Exhibition*, Glassell School of
Art, Houston, TX
Houston Area Exhibition, Blaffer Gallery,
University of Houston, Houston, TX
1995 *A Selection of Contemporary Paintings from
Pakistan*, Pacific Asia Museum, Pasadena,
CA
1992 *New Artists, Recent Works*, Rhotas Gallery,
Islamabad, Pakistan

Vivan Sundaram

Born in 1943, Shimla, India
Lives in New Delhi, India

Vivan Sundaram
HOUSE, 1996

Education
1966   Post-Diploma (Commonwealth Scholar), Slade School of Fine Art, University College London, London, UK
1961   BA, MS University of Baroda, Baroda, India

Selected Solo Exhibitions
1995-96   *The Sher-Gil Archive*, Mücsarnok Dorottya Gallery, Budapest and Hungarian Information and Cultural Centre, Budapest, Hungary (catalogue/touring)
1995   *Riverscape*, Birla Academy of Art and Culture, Calcutta, India (touring)
1994   *Map, Monument, Fallen Mortal, Works from Collaboration/Combines, Riverscape and Memorial*, South London Gallery, London, UK
HOUSE/BOAT, OBORO Gallery, Montreal, Canada (catalogue/touring)
1992   *Collaboration/Combines*, Shridharani Gallery, Delhi, India (touring)
1991   *Engine Oil and Charcoal: Works on Paper*, Faculty of Fine Arts, MS University of Baroda, Baroda, India

Selected Group Exibitions
1997   *Power*, 2nd Kwangju Biennale, Kwangju, South Korea (catalogue)
2nd Johannesburg Biennale, Johannesburg, South Africa
6th Bienal de la Habana, Havana, Cuba
Tryst with Destiny-Art in Modern India 1947-1997, CIMA Calcutta at the Singapore Art Museum, Singapore, Malaysia (catalogue)
1996   *The Second Asia-Pacific Triennial of Contemporary Art*, Queensland Art Gallery, Brisbane, Australia
1995   *Configura-2*, Dialogue of Cultures, Erfurt, Germany
1994   *Hundred Years: From the NGMA Collection*, National Gallery of Modern Art, Delhi, India
1993   *A Critical Difference: Contemporary Art from India*, Chapter Art Centre, Cardiff, Wales, UK (catalogue/touring)
1991   *4th Bienal de la Habana*, Havana, Cuba
1985   *The 2nd Asian Art Show*, Fukuoka Museum, Fukuoka, Japan
1981   *Place for People*, Jehangir Art Gallery, Bombay, India

Bibliography

Ayisha Abraham

By artist

Abraham, Ayisha. "Response to 'Questions of Feminism." *October* 72 (Spring 1995): 6.

_____. "Black Male: Reframing Race in America at Whitney Museum." *World Art* 2 (Winter 1994-95): 21.

_____. "Redefining the Diaspora." *Rungh Magazine* 2, no.4 (Fall 1994): 17.

_____. *Godzilla Newsletter* (Fall 1994): 2.

About artist

Mathur, Chandan. "Migration of Memory." *Samar* 1 (Winter 1992).

Mathur, Saloni. "Revisualizing the Missionary Subject: History, Modernity and Indian Women." *Third Text* 37 (Winter 1996-97): 53.

Rina Banerjee

Cotter, Holland. "Domestic Images from Young Talent." *New York Times*, 10 January 1997, A22.

Kelly, Deirdre. "Indian Girls displays frame of mind." *Globe and Mail*, 12 June 1997.

Pablo Bartholomew

Reena, Jana. "Contemporary Tales from India." *Asian Art News* 7, no.5 (Sept.-Oct. 1997): 92-93.

Zarina Bhimji

By artist

Bhimji, Zarina. "She Loved to Breathe Pure Silence." *Third Text* 3, 4 (Spring-Summer 1988): 96-104.

About artist

Bonami, Francesco. "Spot Light: no place (like home)." *Flash Art* 13, no. 195 (Summer 1997): 131.

Bradley, Jill. "An Audience unto Herself." *Women's Art* 51 (Mar.-Apr. 1993): 23.

Caniglia, Julie. "no place (like home)." *Artforum* 35, no. 10 (Summer 1997): 142-43.

Jones, Kellie. "In Her Own Image." *Artforum* 29, no. 3 (Nov. 1990): 132-38.

Rangsamy, Jacques. "Confrontation." *Third Text* 22 (Spring 1993): 79-86.

Chila Kumari Burman

Cheddie, Janice. "Body Rites: The Self-portraits of Chila Burman." *Women's Art Magazine* 49 (1992).

deSouza, Allan. "Body Weapons." *Camerawork* 34 (1994): 30.

Esders, Viviane. "Our Mothers." *Portraits by 72 Women Photographers*. New York: Stewart, Tabori & Chang, 1996, 36-37.

Golding, Sue. *The Eight Technologies of Otherness.* London: Routledge, 1997, 69-72.

Hagiwara, Hiroko. *Black Women Artists Speak Out.* Osaka: BQ Books, 1990, 149-86.

Meskimmon, Martha. "Women Artists: Self-Portrait in the 20th Century." *The Art of Reflection.* London: Scarlet Press, 1996, 194.

Nead, Lynda. *Chila Kumari Burman: Beyond Two Cultures.* London: Kala Press, 1995.

Nead, Lynda. *The Female Nude: Art, Obscenity, and Sexuality.* London: Routledge, 1992, 70-74.

Parker, Ruzika, and Griselda Pollock. *Art and the Women's Movement 1970-1985.* London: Pandora Press, 1987, 64-67, 328-29.

Rangsamy, Jacques. "Confrontation." *Third Text* 22 (Spring 1993): 79-86.

Sebastian, Amanda. "Evidence to the Point." *Women's Art Magazine* (1996): 26-28.

Ugwu, Catherine. *Lets Get It On: The Politics of Black Performance.* London: ICA Publication; Seattle: Bay Press, 1995, 112-18.

Mohini Chandra

Brittain, David. *Creative Camera* 343 (Dec.-Jan. 1997): 4-5.

Fox, Anna. "School is Out: New Photography by Women." *Women's Art Magazine* 59 (Summer 1994): 34-35.

Holder, Jo. "Africus." *Eyeline* 28 (Spring 1995).

Nayar, D. "When Pictures Tell Tales." *India Mail*, 19-25 April 1996.

Usherwood, P. "Occupying Territories." *Art Monthly* 181 (Nov. 1994): 31.

Poulomi Desai

McMullan, James. "Paloumi." [sic] *Dazed & Confused*, (June 1996).

Allan deSouza

By artist

deSouza, Allan. "Biology Lessons." *Strange Fruit.* Los Angeles: LA Center for Photographic Studies, 1995.

_____. "Dirt." *Asiam* 1 (1997).

_____. "The Flight of/from the Primitive." *Third Text* 38 (Spring 1997): 65-79.

_____. "Going Native." *Trophies of Empire.* Hull: Bluecoat/Arnolfini Galleries, 1994.

_____. "An Imperial Legacy." *Crossing Black Waters.* London: Working Press, 1992, 6-8.

_____. "Once Bitten." *Amerasia Journal* 22, no. 1 (1996): 239-46.

_____. "Notes on the Margins of the White Body." *Naked Truths.* Honolulu: University of Hawaii, 1996.

_____. "Portrait of the Artist as a Dirty Young Man." *Ecstatic Antibodies.* Edited by Tessa Boffin and Sunil Gupta. London: Rivers Oram Press, 1990.

_____. "Re-Placing Angels (extrants and extractions)." *Tracing Culture.* New York: Whitney Museum, 1994.

_____. "Return to Bhowani Junction." *Amerasia Journal* 23, no.2 (1997):124-39.

_____. "Sushi Deluxe: Star Trek, Oedipus and the Native Informant." *New Observations* 107 (1995): 26-27.

_____. "The Spoken Word." *Third Text* 24 (1993): 73-79.

_____. "Stories to Read Aloud" and extract from "Re-Placing Angels." *On a Bed of Rice.* Edited by Geraldine Kudaka. New York: Doubleday, 1995.

_____. "Sublime Differences." *Distinguishing Marks.* London: Institute of Education, 1990.

About artist

Alemayehu, Louis. "Interrogating Identity." *Artpaper* 11, no. 6 (1992): 13.

Chayat, Sherry. *Syracuse Herald American*, 27 April 1997, 14.

Cotter, Holland, "This Realm of Newcomers, This England." *New York Times*, 24 October 1997, 29.

Fusco, Coco. *English is Broken Here.* New York: The New Press, 34.

Lippard, Lucy. *The Pink Glass Swan.* New York: The New Press, 1995, 34.

Slang, Jade. (interview) *Asian American Arts Dialogue* 3, no.4 (1994).

Atul Dodiya

Dalmia, Yashodhara. *Indian Contemporary Art: Post Independence.* New Delhi: Vadhera Gallery, 1997.

Hoskote, Ranjit. "Interim Reports" *Atul Dodiya: Oil Paintings.* Bombay: Gallery Chemould, 1995.

_____. "Evoking the Silence of Dawn." *Interiors India.* Bombay: Indian and Engineering Company Ltd. and IBM Publishers Pvt. Ltd., 1991.

Khakhar, Bhupen. "A Dialogue." *Atul Dodiya: New Paintings.* Calcutta: CIMA Gallery, 1997.

Patel, Gieve. Untitled essay in untitled exhibition brochure. Bombay: Gallery Chemould, 1989.

Tuli, Neville. *The Flamed Mosaic: Contemporary Indian Painting.* Ahmedabad: Mapin Publishing, Pvt. Ltd., 1997.

Sunil Gupta

By artist

Gupta, Sunil. "Memory, History and Language: The Works of Dominique Blain." *Dominique Blain.* Bristol: Arnolfini, 1997.

_____. "Culture Wars: Race and Queer Art." *Outlooks: Lesbian and Gay Sexualities and Visual Culture.* Edited by Peter Horne and Reina Lewis. London: Routledge, 1996, 170-71.

_____. "India Postcard." *Queer Looks.* Edited by John Greyson, Martha Gever, Pratibha Parmer. New York and London: Routledge, 1993.

_____. "Introduction." *Disrupted Borders.* Edited by Sunil Gupta. London: Rivers Oram Press, 1993.

_____. "No Solution." *Ecstatic Antibodies.* Edited by Tessa Boffin and Sunil Gupta. London: Rivers Oram Press, 1990, 103-11.

About artist

Carver, Antonia. "Getting Them between the Eyes: An Interview with Sunil Gupta." *ARTAsia Pacific* 16 (1997).

"Sunil Gupta." *Creative Camera* 339 (Apr.-May 1996).

"TRESPASS 2." *Exposure* 29, nos. 2, 3 (1994).

Permindar Kaur

Andrews, Jorelle. "Re-negotiating the Familiar, Inhabiting the Strange: The Installations of Permindar Kaur." *Crosscurrents.* Oslo: Museum of Ethnography, 1997.

Chambers, Eddie. "Cold Comfort." *Third Text* 36 (Fall 1996): 91-94.

Cork, Richard. "British Art Show 4." *British Art Show.* London: South Bank Centre, 1995, 29-30.

Glass, Stuart. "Cot." *Alice Magazine* 1 (Aug. 1997): 51.

Juncosa, Enrique. "Las Nuevas Confesiónes." *El Pais* (Mar. 1994).

Masterson, Piers. "Cold Comfort." *Arts Monthly* 198 (Jul.-Aug. 1996): 33-34.

Proctor, Nancy. "Is Women's Art Homeless?" *Women's Art Magazine* 71 (Aug.-Sept. 1996): 10-11.

Vijay Kumar

Datta, Jyotirmoy. "50 Artists' Exhibition Honors Jubilee." *India Abroad*, 27 June 1997, 7.

Desmet, Anne, RE. "A Slice of Artistic Life in the Big Apple." *Bankside Bulletin* 18 (Spring 1997): 1-2.

"'India Portfolio' The Hatreds of India." *Earth Times*, 16-31 August 1997, 10-14.

Melwani, Lavina. "Colors of Nostalgia." *India Today*, 15 March 1996, 64 d-g.

"Vijay Kumar." *The Print Collector's Newsletter* 24, no. 5 (Nov.-Dec. 1993): 186.

"Vijay Kumar's 'India Portfolio'." *Flash Art* 29, no. 186 (Jan.-Feb. 1996): 38.

Nalini Malani

Gokhale, Shanta. *Under the Skin.* Bombay: Gallery 7, 1990.

Kapoor, Kamala. "Container '96: Art Across Oceans." *Art News Magazine of India*, (Mumbai), 1996.

_____. "Container '96: Art Across Oceans." *ARTAsia Pacific* 14 (1997): 34-37.

_____. "Missives from the Streets: The Art of Nalini Malani." *ARTAsia Pacific* 2, no.1 (1995): 41-51.

_____. "Memory, Stress, Recall." *Expressions and Evocations: Contemporary Women Artists of India.* Mumbai: Marg Publications, 1996.

_____. *Body as Gesture.* New Delhi: India International Centre, 1995.

Kurian, Pramila. *The Human Factor.* Bombay: Pundole Art Gallery, 1986.

Rajadhyaksha, Ashish. *The City of Desires.* Bombay: Sakshi Gallery, 1991.

_____. "On Mueller's Medea." *Heiner Mueller's Medea.* Bombay: Max Mueller Bhavan, 1993.

Shaheen Merali

Carty, Peter. "Changing Jobs." *The Guardian*, 24 April 1996.

Clark, Robert. "The Evidence Room." *The Guardian*, 10 October 1995.

de Souza, Allan. "The Flight of/from the Primitive." *Third Text* 38 (1997): 65-79.

_____. "Knocking the Door." *Creative Camera* 319 (Dec.-Jan. 1993): 48-49.

Guha, Tania. "Channels, Echoes and Empty Chairs." *Time Out* (London) (Oct. 19-26, 1994): 44.

Jecchinis, Kieron. "Achilles Heels." *Men and Masculinities*. (Winter-Spring 1997): 38.

Kossof, Julian. "Strange Conviction." *Time Out* (London), (Dec. 4-11, 1996): 26.

Petry, Michael, ed. *Art and Design* 47 (1997): 17, 85.

Nasreen Mohamedi

Altaf, ed. *Nasreen in Retrospect*. Bombay: Ashraf Mohamedi Trust, 1995.

Shani Mootoo

By artist

Mootoo, Shani. *Out on Main Street: A Collection of Short Fiction*. Vancouver: Press Gang Publishers, 1997.

_____. *Cereus Blooms at Night*. Vancouver: Press Gang Publishers, 1996.

Samena Rana

Gupta Sunil, ed. *Disrupted Borders: An Intervention in Definitions of Borders*. London: Rivers Oram Press, 1993, 166-73.

Navin Rawanchaikul

Chanjarean, Chanyaporn. "Strange Encounters." *Artlink* 13, nos. 3,4 (Dec. 1993-Jan.1994): 32.

Chanrochanakit, Bandit. "New Generations with Creation and Appreciation in Culture." *GM Magazine* 10, no.149 (Jul. 1995): 138-46.

Chapakdee, Thanom. "Negative Shock." *Bangkok Metro Magazine* 9 (Apr. 1995): 71.

Kirker, Anne. "Navin Rawanchaikul's Social Research." *ARTAsia Pacific* 3, no. 4 (Oct.-Dec. 1996): 70-77.

Knithichan, Khetsirin. "Substance is Intended to Shock." *The Nation*, 19 January 1995, Arts Focus, C8.

Pongsuwan, Siwaporn. "There Is No Voice for People Like Navin." *Thailand Times* 1, no. 151 (March 1994): Sec. C.

Rubinstein, Raphael. "Art by the (Taxi) Meter." *Art in America* 85, no.1 (Jan. 1997): 23.

Ushiroshoji, Masahiro. "Artist Interview: Navin Rawanchaikul." *BT* 48, no.729 (Aug. 1996): 104-13.

Ravinder G. Reddy

Cotter, Holland. "The Brave New Force of Art from the Past." *New York Times*, 29 September 1996, Sec. 2.

Desai, Vishakha N. "The Asia Society Traditions and Tensions." *ARTAsia Pacific* 4, no. 4 (1996): 99.

Karle, Marta. "Stylised Indianness to Raw Immediacy." *Indian Contemporary Art Post Independence*. New Delhi: Vadhera Art Gallery, 1997, 244-45.

Kent, Sarah. "Worlds Apart." *Time Out* (London) (June 1993).

Singh, Ajay. "Transfiguring the Ritual Body." *Art News Magazine of India*, 2 (Oct. 1997): 79-81.

Sircar, Anjali. "Affirmation of Life." *Contemporary Art in Baroda*. Edited by Gulae Mohammed Sheik. New Delhi: Tulika, 1997, 204-206.

N. N. Rimzon

By artist

Rimzon, N.N. "The Artist as Exile: A Note by the Sculptor." *Art Heritage* 10 (1991): 20-21.

About artist

Bhushan, Rasna. "This Conundrum: the Sculpture of N.N. Rimzon." *India Magazine* (Oct. 1991).

Kapur, Geeta. "One Hundred Years from the National Gallery of Modern Art Collection: Working Notes." *ARTAsia Pacific* 2, no. 1 (Nov. 1995): 82-86.

_____. "When Was Modernism an Indian Art?" *Arts and Ideas* 27, 28 (Mar. 1995): 104-26.

Lynn, Victoria. "Between the Pot and the Sword: The Art of N.N. Rimzon." *ARTAsia Pacific* 3, no. 2 (Apr. 1996): 86-89.

Panikkar, Shivaji, and Dagupta Ansuhuman. "The Transitional Modern: Figuring the Post-Modern in Indian Art." *Lalit Kala Contemporary* 41 (1995).

Satish Sharma

By artist

Sharma, Satish. "Cartier-Bresson: The Maestro of Candid Camera." *Sunday Observer*, 15 November 1992.

_____. "Dreams that Money Can Buy." *Creative Camera* 325 (Dec.-Jan. 1994).

_____. "Hidden Histories: The Colonial Encounter." *A Shifting Focus: Photography in India, 1850-1900*. New Delhi: National Gallery of Modern Art, 1995.

_____. *Homai Vyarawalla*. New Delhi: Max Mueller Bhavan, 1993.

_____. "Framing Magical Moments Seized from the Flow of Life." *Economic Times*, 12 September 1993.

About artist

Bharucha, Rustom. *In the Name of the Secular*. New Delhi: *Oxford University Press*, 1998.

Bhattacharya, Santawana. "Framing the Framers." *Indian Express*, 3 October 1997.

_____. "Photo Identity." *Express Magazine*, 8 September 1996.

Morparia, Hemant. "Images From the Real World." *The Independent*, 11 September 1990.

Shinde, Niyatee. "Not To Be Laughed At." *Times of India*, 9 September 1990.

Shahzia Sikander

Baker, Kenneth. "Uprooted." *San Francisco Chronicle*, 22 May 1997.

Friis-Hansen, Dana. "Full Blown – (The Expansive Vision of Minaturist Shahzia Sikander) –" *ARTAsia Pacific* 16 (Fall 1997): 44-49.

Hashmi, Salima. "Fine Art." *Newsline* (Apr. 1996).

Jana, Reena. "Cultural Weaving." *Asian Art News* 7, no. 2 (Mar.-Apr. 1997): 86-87.

Lutfy, Carol. "Asian Artists In America: Shahzia Sikander." *Atelier* 832 (Dec. 1996): 49-58.

MacAdam, Barbara A. "Review: Whitney Biennial." *ARTnews* 96, no.5 (May 1997): 163.

Sirmans, Franklin. "Review: Selections Spring '97 at the Drawing Center." *Flash Art*, 30, 194 (May 1997): 75.

Smith, Roberta. "Drawing that Pushes Beyond the Boundaries." *New York Times*, 21 March 1997.

Dayanita Singh

By artist

Singh, Dayanita, "Mother India." *Granta* 57 (Spring 1997): 221-33.

About artist

Alibhai-Brown, Yasmin. "Inside Story." *Independent Magazine*, 9 September 1997, 18-24.

Cotter, Holland. "Visions of India: Sensual and Stark." *New York Times*, 28 July 1997, C24.

Morparia, Hemant, "The Mind's Eye." *Art News Magazine of India* 2, no. 2 (Oct. 1997): 61.

Reena, Jana. "Contemporary Tales from India." *Asian Art News* 7, no.5 (Sept.-Oct. 1997): 92-93.

Vivan Sundaram

Ananth, Deepak. "Storm Over Asia." *ARTAsia Pacific* 12, no. 1 (1995): 53-61.

Bhabha, Homi K. "Halfway House." *Artforum* 35, no. 9 (May 1997): 11-12, 125.

Nagy, Peter. "The Sher-Gil Archive." *Grand Street* 16, no. 2 (1997): 73.

Petherbridge, Deanna. *The Riverscape Project: Art and Regeneration*. Cleveland: Cleveland Arts, 1994, 5-16.

Roberts, John. "Indian Art Identity and the Avant-Garde: Sculpture of Vivan Sundaram." *Third Text* 27 (1994): 31- 36.

Homai Vyarawalla

Anant, Victor. *India: A Celebration of Independence 1947-1997*. Afterword by Ann D'Harnoncourt and Michael E. Hoffman. New York: Aperture, and Philadelphia: Philadelphia Museum of Art, 1997.

"Art That Changed with the Time." *The Statesman*, 9 October 1993, 2.

"Delhi, May 14, 1951." *The Statesman*, 116, no. 24267.

Joshi, Amitabh. "The Grand Old Lady of Photojournalism." *Asian Photography*, 6 October 1993, 4.

Karaka, Ratan. "India's Best-Known Woman Photographer Too Missed the World's Greatest News Picture." *Current* (1961): 3-4.

Kavaran, Roxanne. "Mother of Press Photography." *Sunday Times of India*, 14 February 1993, 5.

_____. "Remembrance of Faces Past." *Sunday Times of India*, 7 August 1994, 12.

_____. "Vyarawalla in Focus." *Parsiana* (Oct. 1992): 28-30.

Marather, Kaumudi. "History on a Bromide." *Marquee*, 3 August 1994, 7.

Menon, Sadanand. "Honouring the 'Mother' of Indian Photographers." *Economic Times*, New Delhi, 12 September 1993, 12.

Misra, R.K. "First Lady of Indian Photography." *The Pioneer*, 13 April 1994, 15.

Nair, B. Pradeep. "She Spared None–Shot Them All!" *Indian Express*, 14 December 1993, 5.

Niyatee. "The Images of Homai." *Indian Express*, 7 August 1994, 7.

Pestonji, P. "Shades of Grey." *Times of India*, 7 August 1994, VI.

Prasad, Krishna. "A Quirk of the Light–and She Missed the Shot of the Century." *Sunday Observer*, 7-13 August 1994, 1-2.

Sharma, Anju. "Homai Vyarawalla's People." *Times of India*, 9 September 1993.

Sharma, Satish. "Framing Magical Moments Seized from the Flow of Life." *Economic Times*, New Delhi, 12 September 1993, 12.

_____. "Woman Who Shot Them All." *Economic Times*, 31 May 1992, 16.

"She Kept Makers of History in Focus." *Indian Express*, 25 September 1993, cameo page.

Singh, Kavita. "Pictures of Pure Charm." *Indian Express Sunday Magazine*, 28 June 1992, 4, 11.

Zarina

Borum, Jenifer P. "Asia/America." *Artforum* 33, no.1 (Sept. 1994): 108.

Glowen, Ron. "Matters of Survival: Asia/America." *Artweek* 25 (Nov. 3, 1994): 14.

Hirch, Fay. "Zarina Hashmi." *On Paper* 2, no.2 (Nov.-Dec. 1997): 41.

Liebmann, Lisa. "Zarina's Balm: Objects of Exchange." *Artforum* 26 (Jan. 1988): 74-76.

Nadelman, Cynthia. "New Editions: Zarina Hashmi." *ARTnews* 81, no.7 (1982): 77.

Safrani, Shehbaz M. "Zarina at the Bronx Museum of the Arts." *Asian Art News* 2, no.2 (Mar.-Apr. 1992).

Checklist of Exhibition

Dimensions are in inches unless otherwise noted; height precedes width.

Ayisha Abraham
(Bangalore, India)
…looks the other way: Balcony Men,
1993-94
Computer-generated color
  photograph, 30 x 20"
Collection of the artist

…looks the other way: Boots, 1993-94
Computer-generated color
  photograph on Masonite, 20 x 24"
Collection of the artist

…looks the other way: Crossed Legs
  with Hat, 1993-94
Computer-generated color
  photograph, 20 x 24"
Collection of the artist

…looks the other way: the Doll,
1993-94
Computer-generated color
  photograph on Masonite, 20 x 40"
Collection of the artist

…looks the other way: the Doll,
1993-94
Computer-generated color
  photograph on Masonite, 20 x 40"
Collection of the artist

…looks the other way: the Doll,
1993-94
Computer-generated color
  photograph on Masonite, 20 x 40"
Collection of the artist

…looks the other way: Eyes, 1993-94
Computer-generated color
  photograph, 20 x 24"
Collection of the artist

…looks the other way: Hats and
  Umbrella, 1993-94
Computer-generated color
  photograph on Masonite, 20 x 24"
Collection of the artist

…looks the other way: …looks the other
  way, 1993-94
Computer-generated color
  photograph on Masonite, 20 x 30"
Collection of the artist

…looks the other way: …looks the other
  way, 1993-94
Computer-generated color
  photograph on Masonite, 20 x 30"
Collection of the artist

…looks the other way: …looks the other
  way, 1993-94
Computer-generated color
  photograph on Masonite, 20 x 24"
Collection of the artist

Rina Banerjee
(State College, PA, and Brooklyn, NY)
Home within a Harem, 1997
Mixed media installation
Dimensions variable
Collection of the artist

Pablo Bartholomew
(New Delhi, India)
Indians in America: Bridegroom with
  Family in the Back Lot of a Hired
  Church Building, Connecticut, 1988
Color photograph, 16 x 20"
Collection of the artist

Indians in America: Farm Workers
  Eating Parathas and Achar during
  Lunch Hour, Yuba, California, 1988
Color photograph, 16 x 20"
Collection of the artist

Indians in America: Indians on Float
  with U.S. Flag and Message Voicing
  Concerns about Amendment to
  Immigration Law, India Day Parade,
  Manhattan, NYC, 1988
Color photograph, 16 x 20"
Collection of the artist

Indians in America: A Jain Acharya
  with His Fellow Eating Tacos in
  Upstate New York, 1988
Color photograph, 16 x 20"
Collection of the artist

Indians in America: Last Viewing of a
  Punjabi Woman in a Funeral Parlor,
  El Centro, California, 1988
Color photograph, 16 x 20"
Collection of the artist

Indians in America: South Asian
  Muslims Pray during Id at Corona
  Park, Flushing Meadows, Queens,
  New York, 1988
Color photograph, 16 x 20"
Collection of the artist

Zarina Bhimji
(London, UK)
It is Like a Brightness in the Heart, 1997
Cibachrome transparency in light box,
  34 1/2 x 41 1/2 x 71 1/4"
Collections of Bradford Art Galleries
  and Museums, Bradford, UK,
  commissioned in collaboration with
  Institute of International Visual
  Arts (INIVA)

Chila Kumari Burman
(London, UK)
Dad on Ship Coming to Britain, Mum
  and the Queens, and Dad's Ice-Cream
  Van on the Beach, 1995
Cibachrome print, 23 x 12"
Collection of the artist
Courtesy of Autograph, London, UK

Me and Sister Ashra — Ashra in the
  Pram and Ashok in the Street— in
  Bootle in the 60s, 1995
Cibachrome print, 23 x 12"
Collection of the artist
Courtesy of Autograph, London, UK

Fly Girl Watching the World,
  Auto-Portrait, 1993
Mixed media and laser print, 65 x 40"'
Collection of the artist

Hard Times — Dad and Me and Ashok
  in the Kitchen, 1995
Cibachrome print, 23 x 12"
Collection of the artist
Courtesy of Autograph, London, UK

Portrait of My Mother, Sweet Flower,
  Mummyji; Mixed Media: Heart,
  Liver, Kidney, Earth, Fire, Water,
  Metal, 1995
Cibachrome print, 23 x 12"
Collection of the artist
Courtesy of Autograph, London, UK

Mohini Chandra
(London, UK)
Album Pacifica, 1997
100 photographs; each approximately
  8 x 10"
Collection of the artist

Poulomi Desai
(London, UK)
Shakti Queens: Mithu and Nargis, 1996
Color photograph, 30 x 22"
Collection of the artist
Courtesy of Autograph, London, UK

Shakti Queens: Shakuntala Devi and
  Dimple, 1997
Color photograph, 30 x 22"
Collection of the artist
Courtesy of Autograph, London, UK

Shakti Queens: Vijiya Devi and Meena,
1997
Color photograph, 30 x 22"
Collection of the artist
Courtesy of Autograph, London, UK

Shakti Queens: Princess Aaliyah and
  Hema, 1997
Color photograph, 22 x 30"
Collection of the artist
Courtesy of Autograph, London, UK

Allan deSouza
(Los Angeles, CA)
American Indian: Taj Mahal, 1997
C-print, 16 x 16"
Collection of the artist

American Indian: Taj Mahal, 1997
C-print, 16 x 16"
Collection of the artist

American Indian: Taj Mahal, 1997
C-print, 16 x 16"
Collection of the artist

American Indian: Jungle Cruise, 1997
C-print, 16 x 16"
Collection of the artist

American Indian: Jungle Cruise, 1997
C-print, 16 x 16"
Collection of the artist

American Indian: Monument to
  the Discoveries, 1997
C-print, 16 x 16"
Collection of the artist

American Indian: Monument to
  the Discoveries, 1997
C-print, 16 x 16"
Collection of the artist

Lady Asia, 1997
C-print, 27 x 39"
Collection of the artist

Threshold: Dulles, 1997
C-print, 16 x 16"
Collection of the artist

Threshold: JFK, 1997
C-print, 16 x 16"
Collection of the artist

Threshold: LAX, 1997
C-print, 16 x 16"
Collection of the artist

Threshold: Lisbon, 1997
C-print, 16 x 16"
Collection of the artist

Threshold: Lisbon, 1997
C-print, 16 x 16"
Collection of the artist

Threshold: O'Hare, 1997
C-print, 16 x 16"
Collection of the artist

Threshold: Union Station, 1997
C-print, 16 x 16"
Collection of the artist

Atul Dodiya
(Ghat Kopar, near Mumbai
  [formerly Bombay], India)
"Hand Me Your Keys" (Durga), 1994
Oil on canvas, 69 x 48"
Collection of Ms. R. Sarkar, CIMA,
  Calcutta, India

2nd October, 1993
Oil on canvas, 64 x 48"
Collection of Chester and
  Davida Herwitz

Sunday Morning, Marine Drive, 1995
Oil and acrylic on canvas, 60 x 84"
Collection of RPG Enterprise

Sunil Gupta
(London, UK)
Selections from *TRESPASS 3,* 1995
14 digital inkjet prints
Dimensions variable
Collection of the artist
Nos. 54, 56, 59, 60, Collections of
  Bradford Art Galleries and
  Museums, Bradford, UK

Mariam Ishaque
(New York, NY)
Bachelor's Travels I, 1995
Egg tempera on panel, 12 x 24"
Collection of the artist

Bachelor's Travels II, 1995
Egg tempera on panel, 12 x 9"
Collection of the artist

Hide and Seek, 1996
Egg tempera and collage on
  panel, 12 x 9"
Collection of the artist

Flat-Footed Traveler, 1996
Egg tempera and collage on panel,
 16 x 12"
Collection of the artist

No Pain, No Gain II, 1995
Egg tempera on panel, 12 x 9"
Collection of the artist

Permindar Kaur
(London, UK)
Falling, 1995
Polar fleece and arctic fur
76 figures; each approximately 4 x 5 x 1"
Collection of the artist

Vijay Kumar
(Brooklyn, NY)
India Portfolio, 1993
18 etchings with photograph etching,
 12 x 16" each
Collection of the artist

Nalini Malani
(Mumbai [formerly Bombay], India)
Betrayal, 1993
Watercolor on paper, 22 1/2 x 30"
Collection of Chester and
 Davida Herwitz

Control, 1993
Watercolor on paper, 22 1/2 x 30"
Collection of Chester and
 Davida Herwitz

Mutant, undated
Acrylic, charcoal, and conte on
 paper, 28 x 35 1/2"
Collection of Chester and
 Davida Herwitz

Shaheen Merali
(London, UK)
Going Native, 1992
Canvas deck chairs, videotape,
 audiotape, and projected slides
Dimensions variable
Collection of the artist

Nasreen Mohamedi
(Vadodara [formerly Baroda],
 Gujarat, India; deceased 1990)
Untitled, undated
Pen and ink on paper, 20 x 28 1/2"
Collection of Chester and
 Davida Herwitz

Untitled, undated
Pen and ink on paper, 23 1/2 x 29 1/2"
Collection of Chester and
 Davida Herwitz

Untitled, undated
Pen and ink on paper, 20 1/2 x 20 1/2"
Collection of Chester and
 Davida Herwitz

Untitled, undated
Pen and ink on paper, 23 x 29"
Collection of Chester and
 Davida Herwitz

Untitled, undated.
Pen and ink on paper, 20 x 26 1/2"
Collection of Chester and
 Davida Herwitz

Shani Mootoo
(Vancouver, Canada)
A Landscape of One's Own, 1995
Color photocopies,
 approximately 61 x 44"
Collection of the artist

The Urbanites' Fiction, 1996
Photographic work composed of
 174 color photographs, 79 x 53 1/2"
Collection of the artist

Samena Rana
(London, UK; deceased 1992)
Four photographs from *Flow of
 Water*, 1990
C-type color photographs, each 17
 1/2 x 24 3/4" (framed dimensions)
Collection of Panchayat, London, UK

Navin Rawanchaikul
(Chiang Mai, Thailand, and
 Fukuoka, Japan)
*from Chiang Mai on September 28,
 1997*
Installation, postcards, postcard rack,
 and telephone. Room dimensions:
 15' 31/2" x 18'10"; rack: 57 x 9 x 9";
 telephone approximately 9 x 7 3/4"
Collection of the artist

Ravinder G. Reddy
(Visakhapatnam, India)
Family, 1997
Polyester-resin fiberglass,
 gilt, and paint, 42 x 82 x 52"
Collection of the artist

Krishna Veni, 1997
Polyester-resin fiberglass,
 gilt, and paint, 76 x 75 x 74"
Collection of the artist

N. N. Rimzon
(Trivandrum, Southern India)
*Faraway from One Hundred and
 Eight Feet*, 1995
108 terra-cotta pots, straw, and rope
Dimensions variable
Collection of the artist

Satish Sharma
(New Delhi, India)
10 photographs from *Deconstructing
 the Politician*, 1990-96
Black-and-white photographs
Dimensions variable
Collection of the artist

Shahzia Sikander
(Lahore, Pakistan, and Houston, TX)
Uprooted, 1995
Vegetable color, dry pigment,
 watercolor, and tea on *wasli*
 (handmade paper), 8 1/2 x 7 1/4"
Collection of Aliya Hasan

Uprooted Order Series 3, no. 1, 1997
 Vegetable color, dry pigment,
 watercolor, and tea on *wasli*
 (handmade paper), 6 7/16 x 3 1/2"
 Collection of Joseph Havel

Uprooted Order Series 3, no. 2, 1997
 Vegetable color, dry pigment, and
 watercolor on *wasli* (handmade
 paper), 13 1/8 x 9 1/2"
 Collection of Jacquelyn and Bruce
 Brown

Dayanita Singh
(New Delhi, India)
*All the Women of the Guptoos Family
 in Their Traditional Saris*, 1997
Black-and-white photograph, 16 x 20"
Collection of the artist

*Bina Rao's Family Meet for Evening
 Tea in Her Bangalore Apartment*, 1997
Black-and-white photograph, 16 x 20"
Collection of the artist

*Dolly Jabbar in Her Colonial Calcutta
 Home*, 1997
Black-and-white photograph, 16 x 20"
Collection of the artist

*The Guptoos are a Large Traditional
 Joint Family in Calcutta.
 Grandparents are Still Heads of the
 Family*, 1997
Black-and-white photograph, 16 x 20"
Collection of the artist

*Nina Chauhan and Her Daughter
 Practice the Tango, which They Are
 Learning at a Dance*, 1997
Black-and-white photograph, 16 x 20"
Collection of the artist

*Prasad Bedappa and His Daughter and
 Their Two Dogs in Their Apartment
 in Bangalore*, 1997
Black-and-white photograph, 16 x 20"
Collection of the artist

*Rita Dhody and Her Two Daughters
 in Their Sea-Facing Apartment in
 Bombay*, 1997
Black-and-white photograph, 16 x 20"
Collection of the artist

*Samara Chopra and Her Friend Pooja
 Dress Alike for a Photograph Lesson
 and Deen Dayal, the Caretaker, is
 Amazed at How Quickly They Have
 Grown*, 1997
Black-and-white photograph, 16 x 20"
Collection of the artist

*Sybil and Her Daughter Sunanda in
 Their Calcutta Home. In the
 Background a Maid Walks By*, 1997
Black-and-white photograph, 16 x 20"
Collection of the artist

Vivan Sundaram
(New Delhi, India)
HOUSE, 1996
Kalam Kush handmade paper, steel,
 glass, wood, cement, water, oil,
 pigment, television
Approximately 6 x 6 x 6'
Collection of the artist
Courtesy of OBORO Gallery,
 Montreal, Canada

Homai Vyarawalla
(Vadodara [formerly Baroda],
 Gujarat, India)
*After being sworn in as the first
 governor-general of India on 15th
 August, 1947, Lord Mountbatten was
 to be given guard of honour in front of
 the Council Hall, but the serge of
 jubilant people was so great that the
 function had to be abandoned. Picture
 shows him waving at the crowds who
 were shouting for him to show himself.*
Black-and-white photograph,
 15 3/4 x 21 3/4"
Collection of the artist

*The ashes of Mahatma Gandhi were
 immersed in the Triveni River at
 Allahabad by his relatives and
 followers. Among those present on the
 boat carrying the urn were his son
 Devdas, Mrs. Sirojini Naidu (called
 the Nightingale of India), her
 daughter Padmaja, Maulana Azad,
 and Dr. Jeevraj Mehta.*
Black-and-white photograph,
 15 3/8 x 22 1/4"
Collection of the artist

*Dr. Rajendra Prasad became first
 president of Free India in 1950.
 Before going to the Council Hall in
 Delhi to take the oath of office as
 president, he visited Mahatma's
 Samadhi (the place where he had been
 cremated) at Raj Ghat to pay respect
 to Father of the Nation. With him was
 his wife Rajvansi Devi, Sardar Patel,
 and other relatives and friends.*
Black-and-white photograph,
 16 x 22 1/8"
Collection of the artist

*The funeral pyre of Mahatma Gandhi at
 the cremation ground at Raj Ghat,
 Delhi. The religious ceremony was
 officiated by his second son who
 lighted the pyre (January 31, 1948).*
Black-and-white photograph,
 15 3/4 x 22 1/8"
Collection of the artist

*Lord Mountbatten with his wife
 Edwina and daughters Pamella and
 Lady Lumly and his son-in-law paid
 their respects to the Mahatma by
 sitting on bare ground in front of the
 funeral pyre. With them is Raj
 Kumari Amrit Kaur, a staunch
 follower of the Mahatma (January
 31, 1948).*
Black-and-white photograph,
 15 1/16 x 21 7/8"
Collection of the artist

*Crowds gathered on the ramparts of the
 Fort on the 16th August to see Nehru
 and other leaders. Picture shows only
 one-fourth section of the big crowd
 with Jama Masjid on the skyline
 (Delhi).*
Black-and-white photograph,
 15 x 22 3/16"
Collection of the artist

Mahatma Gandhi accompanied by Abdul Ghaffar Khan, popularly known as "Frontier" Gandhi, and Dr. Sushila Nayar, Gandhi's personal physician, arriving at the Congress working committee meeting to discuss 3rd June plan regarding partitioning of India (June 1947).
Black-and-white photograph,
16 1/4 x 19 3/4"
Collection of the artist

Mahatma Gandhi was assassinated on the 30th January, 1948. Picture shows, among others, Mr. Nehru and Lord Mountbatten getting the body ready on the army cortege for the funeral procession in Delhi the next day.
Black-and-white photograph,
15 3/8 x 22 1/8"
Collection of the artist

Mrs. Indira Gandhi on vigil near the body of her father (Pandit Nehru), who died on 27th May, 1964, lying in state at the Prime Minister's residence at Teen Murti Marg, New Delhi.
Black-and-white photograph, 17 x 22"
Collection of the artist

Pandit Nehru addressing the nation as first prime minister of Free India from the ramparts of the Red Fort in Delhi on 16th August, 1947. With him is Deputy Prime Minister Sardar Vallabhbhai Patel (commonly known as the Iron Man of India).
Black-and-white photograph,
18 x 22 1/4"
Collection of the artist

Pandit Nehru while waiting for his sister's arrival at Palam Airport (New Delhi, India, 1954).
Black-and-white photograph,
17 x 17 3/4"
Collection of the artist

Standing on the rampart of the famous Red Fort of Delhi, Pandit Nehru proudly shows Lady Mountbatten the mammoth gathering of joyous people in front of the Red Fort to witness the going-up of India's tricolour flag and to listen to Mr. Nehru addressing the nation as first prime minister of India on 16th of August, 1947.
Black-and-white photograph,
15 1/2 x 22"
Collection of the artist

View of the teeming millions that had gathered in front of the historic Red Fort in Delhi to see the British flag go down and the Tricolour unfurled. (August 16, 1947)
Black-and-white photograph,
15 3/4 x 22 1/4"
Collection of the artist

Women of Delhi gathered in force to garland and felicitate the leaders of the freedom fighters before sending them off to the Council Hall for the declaration of freedom from British rule at midnight of 14th/15th August, 1947. (Pandit Nehru, Sardar Patel and others with garlands.)
Black-and-white photograph,
15 7/8 x 20 7/8"
Collection of the artist

Zarina
(New York, NY)
Homes I Made/A Life in Nine Lines: Bangkok, 1997
Etching with chine collé, 14 x 13"
 plate size; 21 x 19" paper size
Collection of the artist

Homes I Made/A Life in Nine Lines: Bonn, 1997
Etching with chine collé, 14 x 13"
 plate size; 21 x 19" paper size
Collection of the artist

Homes I Made/A Life in Nine Lines: Los Angeles, 1997
Etching with chine collé, 14 x 13"
 plate size; 21 x 19" paper size
Collection of the artist

Homes I Made/A Life in Nine Lines: New Delhi, 1997
Etching with chine collé, 14 x 13"
 plate size; 21 x 19" paper size
Collection of the artist

Homes I Made/A Life in Nine Lines: New Delhi, 1997
Etching with chine collé, 14 x 13"
 plate size; 21 x 19" paper size
Collection of the artist

Homes I Made/A Life in Nine Lines: New York, 1997
Etching with chine collé, 14 x 13"
 plate size; 21 x 19" paper size
Collection of the artist

Homes I Made/A Life in Nine Lines: Paris, 1997
Etching with chine collé, 14 x 13"
 plate size; 21 x 19" paper size
Collection of the artist

Homes I Made/A Life in Nine Lines: Santa Cruz, 1997
Etching with chine collé, 14 x 13"
 plate size; 21 x 19" paper size
Collection of the artist

Homes I Made/A Life in Nine Lines: Tokyo, 1997
Etching with chine collé, 14 x 13"
 plate size; 21 x 19" paper size
Collection of the artist

Somewhere the Flotilla of Sorrow Will Come to Rest, 1997
Installation of 1,001 aluminum
 houses, painted black, each 1 1/2 x
 1 1/4"; total dimensions variable
Collection of the artist

Photographs by Arnold Kanarvogel with exception of:
p. 22, Ayisha Abraham; p. 23, Mohini Chandra; p. 24, courtesy Contemporary Arts Museum, Houston, TX; p. 27, Shaheen Merali; p. 30, Satish Sharma; p. 34, Rina Banerjee; p. 35, Pablo Bartholomew; p. 36, courtesy Bradford Art Galleries and Museums, UK; p. 37, Nick Morris; p.38, Poulomi Desai; p. 39, Allan deSouza; p. 40, Sunil Gupta; p. 43, Shani Mootoo; p. 44, courtesy Panchayat; p. 45, Ravinder G. Reddy; p. 46, N.N. Rimzon; p. 48, Denis Farley, courtesy OBORO Gallery.